The White Indian Boy

Myers, Boise, Idaho

Shoshone Falls of the Snake River, Idaho; one of the wonder scenes in the land of Washakie's tribe.

The
White Indian Boy
The Story of Uncle Nick Among the Shoshones

by

Elijah Nicholas Wilson
"Uncle Nick"

In Collaboration with
Howard R. Driggs
Professor Emeritus of English Education
New York University
President, American Pioneer Trails Association

with drawings by
Perry Driggs

Paragon Press
Salt Lake City, Utah

The number of men and women who played a part in the conquest and settlement of the Great West grows smaller year by year, and the passing of these plainsmen and mountaineers marks the close of an era in our national life. To put into permanent form, as has been done in this book, a pioneer's recollections of his early days, with their trials and adventures, is to make a certain contribution to history. Such a record shows us the courage, perservance, and hardihood with which the foundations of the nation were laid, and to read it is to watch a state in the making. As a story of the days when Indian tribes still roamed the plains, this book will have for boys and girls all the interest of a tale of adventure. It is hoped that it will also give them a realization of the hardships and dangers so manfully faced by the settlers of the West and will implant in them a desire to prove themselves worthy successors to those builders of the nation.

LIBRARY OF CONGRESS CATALOGUE NUMBER 91-067470
ISBN 0-9631605-0-8

1991 Manufactured and Printed in the
United States of America

AN INTRODUCTION TO UNCLE NICK

IF you ever go to the Yellowstone Park by way of Jackson's Hole, you will most likely pass through Wilson, Wyoming. It is a picturesque little village situated at the foot of the Teton Mountains. A clear stream, rightly named Fish Creek, winds its way through the place. On the very edge of this sparkling mountain stream stands a log cabin. The cabin is so near the creek, indeed, that one might stand in the dooryard and catch fish. And this is what "Uncle Nick" Wilson, who lived in the cabin, has done many a time. That is a "true fish story," I am sure, because I caught two lively trout myself last summer in this same creek only a few rods from the cabin.

Who was Uncle Nick Wilson? you ask. He was an old pioneer after whom this frontier town was named. He was the man, too, who wrote this story book. You would have liked Uncle Nick, I know. He was a rather short, round-faced man with a merry twinkle in his eyes. He took things easily; he spoke in a quiet voice; he was never too busy to help his neighbors; he liked a good joke; he was always ready to chat awhile; and he never failed to have a good story to tell, especially to the children.

Uncle Nick had one peculiarity. He did not like to take off his hat, even when he went into a house. I often wondered why, but I did not like to ask him. One day, however, some one told me the reason. It was because he had once been shot in the head with an arrow by an Indian. The scar was still there.

From outward appearances one would hardly have guessed that Uncle Nick's life had been so full of exciting experiences. But when he was sitting about the campfire at night or at the fireside with a group of boys and girls, he would often get to telling his tales of the Indians and the Pony Express; and his hearers would never let him stop. My own two boys never got sleepy when Uncle Nick was in the house; they would keep calling for his stories again and again.

This was one reason why he wrote this story book. He wanted boys and girls to have the pleasure of reading his stories as often as they pleased. How he was induced to write it is an interesting story in itself.

Some years ago two professors of a certain Western university were making a trip with their families to the Yellowstone Park by way of Jackson's Hole trail. As they were passing through Wilson, one of the women in the party met with a serious accident. Her little boy had got among the horses, and the mother, in trying to save the child from harm, was knocked down and trampled.

Help must be had at once; but how to get it was a problem. The nearest doctor was over sixty miles away. While the unfortunate travelers were worrying about what to do, Uncle Nick's wife came to the rescue. She quietly assumed command of affairs, directed the making of a litter, and insisted that the wounded lady be carried to her cabin home a short distance away. Then she turned nurse, dressed the wounds, and attended the sufferer until she was well enough to resume the journey.

The party meantime camped near by, and whiled away about three weeks in fishing and hunting and enjoying Uncle Nick's stories of the Wild West. Every night they would sit about the cabin fire listening to the old frontiersman tell his "Injun stories" and his other thrilling adventures of the early days. They felt that these stories should be written for everybody to enjoy. They were so enthusiastic in their desire to have it done that Uncle Nick finally consented to try to write them.

It was a hard task for him. He had never attended school a day in his life; but his wife had taught him his alphabet, and he had learned to read and spell in some kind of way. He got an old typewriter and set to work. Day by day for several months he clicked away, until most of his stories were told. And here they are — true stories, of real Indians, as our pioneer parents knew them about seventy years ago.

The book gives the nearest and clearest of views of Indian home-life; it is filled, too, with stirring incidents of Indian warfare, of the Pony Express and Overland Stage, and other exciting frontier experiences.

Uncle Nick may have had no schooling except as he got it in the wilds, but he certainly learned how to tell a story well. The charm of his style lies in its Robinson Crusoe simplicity and its touches of Western humor.

Best of all, the stories Uncle Nick tells are true. For many months he was a visitor at our home. To listen to this kindly, honest old man was to believe his words. But the truth of what he tells is proved by the words of many other persons who knew him well, and others who have had similar experiences. For several years I have been proving these stories by talking with other pioneers, mountaineers, pony riders, students of Indian life, and even Indians themselves. Their words have unfailingly borne out the statements of the writer of this book. No pretense is made that this volume is without error. It certainly is accurate, however, in practically every detail, and true to the customs and the spirit of the Indian and pioneer life it portrays.

Professor Franklin T. Baker of Columbia University, who read the book in manuscript, has pronounced the book "a rare find, and a distinctive contribution to the literature that reflects our Western life."

The rugged, kindly man who lived through the scenes herein pictured has passed away. He died at Wilson, the town he founded, in December, 1915, during the seventy-

third year of his age.   But he has left for us this tablet
to his memory, a simple story of a simple man who lived
bravely and cheerily in the storm and stress of earlier days,
taking his part even from boyhood with the full measure
of a man.

Howard R. Driggs

Dedication

To My Father
HOWARD R. DRIGGS

whose firsthand accounts of the early American West have
for a century made epochal reading, and whose own life was
excitingly flavored by the gallant lives of his pioneer fore-
bears, this new edition of an old favorite is affectionately
dedicated.

Perry Driggs

AUTHOR'S FOREWORD

You have no doubt read or heard stories of the great wild West. Perhaps you have even listened to some gray-haired man or woman tell tales of the Indians and the trappers, who roamed over the hills and plains. They may have told you, too, of the daring Pony Express riders who used to go dashing along the wild trails over the prairies and mountains and desert, carrying the mails, and of the Overland men who drove their stages loaded with letters and passengers along the same dangerous roads.

I know something about those stirring early times. More than sixty years of my life have been spent on the Western frontiers, with the pioneers, among the Indians, as a pony rider, a stage driver, a mountaineer, and a ranchman.

I have taken my experiences as they came to me, much as a matter of course, not thinking of them as especially unusual or exciting. Many other men have had similar experiences. They were all bound up in the life we had to live in making the conquest of the West. Others seem, however, to find the stories of my life interesting. My grandchildren and other children, and even grown people, ask me again and again to tell these tales of the earlier days; so I have begun to feel that they may be worth telling and keeping.

That is why I finally decided to write them. It has taken almost more courage to do this than it did actually to live through some of the exciting experiences. I have not had the privilege of attending schools, so it is very hard for me to tell my story with the pen; but perhaps I may be able to give my readers, young and old, some pleasure and help them to get a clearer, truer picture of the real wild West as it was when the pioneers first blazed their way into the land.

"Uncle Nick" Wilson

CONTENTS

PAGE

INTRODUCTION v
    By Howard R. Driggs, telling who Uncle Nick was;
    of his home in Jackson's Hole, Wyoming, and the story
    of how the book came to be written

CHAPTER

1. PIONEER DAYS 1
    A sketch of the pioneer days in the West — Indian
    troubles — Account of desert tribes and Shoshones

2. MY LITTLE INDIAN BROTHER 8
    How Nick learns the Indian language

3. OFF WITH THE INDIANS 12
    Nick joins Washakie's tribe as adopted son of the
    chief's mother — Experience in getting to the tribe

4. THE GREAT ENCAMPMENT 20
    The gathering of the Shoshone nation in Deer Lodge
    Valley, Montana

5. BREAKING CAMP 28
    Story of the Buffalo hunt — Preparing meat for winter

6. VILLAGE LIFE 33
    Winter experiences in the Indian village in Idaho

7. MY INDIAN MOTHER 39
    An Indian mother's sorrow — How she came to want
    a white papoose — Love of the red mother for the
    white child

8. THE CROWS 44
    Struggles of the Shoshones with their rival enemy —
    Scares and war preparation

9. PAPOOSE TROUBLES 57
    Breaking Indian ponies — A fight with bears

10. A LONG JOURNEY 69
    Wanderings of Washakie's tribe through the Idaho
    country on their trip to market their skins and robes

11. THE SNOWY MOONS 79
    Another winter with the Indians — Teaching the
    Indians the ways of the white man — Days of mourn-
    ing

12. THE FIERCE BATTLE 89
    Fight for the buffalo grounds — Description of the
    battle in which Washakie settled the question of
    boundary lines

CHAPTER PAGE

13. LIVELY TIMES 98
An accident — Medicine man doctoring and other
Indian practices in healing

14. OLD MOROGONAI 106
The old Shoshone arrow maker and his stories of early
times — Memories of Lewis and Clark

15. THE BIG COUNCIL 112
Indian chiefs confer as to what shall be done with
the white boy

16. HOMEWARD BOUND 119
Nick, equipped with ponies and Indian trappings,
returns to tell his own story of how he left home

17. THE YEAR OF THE MOVE 128
The coming of Johnston's army to Utah and the
leaving of their homes by the people — Nick shows
his skill at riding wild horses

18. THE PONY EXPRESS 139
Nick chosen as a rider — His experiences carrying the
mail — Shot by an Indian

19. JOHNSTON PUNISHES THE INDIANS 157
Nick as a guide for the United States troops — The
battle in the desert

20. THE OVERLAND STAGE 167
Experiences of Nick as a driver of the Overland

21. A TERRIBLE JOURNEY 176
Establishing the mail route from Idaho to Montana
— The struggle in the snow

22. MY OLD SHOSHONE FRIENDS 192
After experiences with the Indians — Hunting for the
Indian mother's grave — Washakie

23. TRAPPING WITH AN INDIAN 197
Nick spends a winter as a trapper — Description of
the work

24. WORKING ON THE INDIAN RESERVATION . . . 202
Nick in government employ — Troubles in getting
the tribe to settle down

25. FRONTIER TROUBLES 207
Capturing a band of cattle thieves — A chase after
Indian horse-thieves — The Jackson's Hole Indian
trouble — Closing words

GLOSSARY 219

Caspar W. Hodgson

The Teton Peaks from Jackson's Hole, Wyoming.   Jackson's Hole, the last home of Uncle Nick Wilson, is situated in a hunting ground which is famous even yet.   It was named after Jackson, an old trapper.

The Western trail in the early days.

1 PIONEER DAYS

I WAS born in Illinois in 1842. I crossed the plains by
ox team and came to Utah in 1850. My parents settled
in Grantsville, a pioneer village just south of the Great
Salt Lake. To protect themselves from the Indians, the
settlers grouped their houses close together and built a
high wall all around them. Some of the men would
stand guard while others worked in the fields. The
cattle had to be herded very closely during the day, and
corralled at night with a strong guard to keep them from
being stolen. But even with all our watchfulness we lost
a good many of them. The Indians would steal in and
drive our horses and cows away and kill them. Sometimes they killed the people, too.

We built a log schoolhouse in the center of our fort,
and near it we erected a very high pole, up which we could
run a white flag as a signal if the Indians attempted to
run off our cattle, or attack the town or the men in the
fields. In this log schoolhouse two old men would stay,
taking turns at watching and giving signals when neces-

sary, by raising the flag in the daytime, or by beating a drum at night. For we had in the schoolhouse a big bass drum to rouse the people, and if the Indians made a raid, one of the guards would thump on the old thing.

When the people heard the drum, all the women and children were supposed to rush for the schoolhouse and the men would hurry for the cow corral or take their places along the wall. Often in the dead hours of the night when we were quietly sleeping, we would be startled by the booming old drum. Then you would hear the youngsters coming and squalling from every direction. You bet I was there too. Yes, sir, many is the time I have run for that old schoolhouse clinging to my mother's apron and bawling "like sixty"; for we all expected to be filled with arrows before we could get there. We could not go outside of the wall without endangering our lives, and when we would lie down at night we never knew what would happen before morning.

The savages that gave us the most trouble were called Gosiutes. They lived in the deserts of Utah and Nevada. Many of them had been banished into the desert from other tribes because of crimes they had committed. The Gosiutes were a mixed breed of good and bad Indians.

They were always poorly clad. In the summer they went almost naked; but in winter they dressed themselves in robes made by twisting and tying rabbit skins together. These robes were generally all they had to wear during the day and all they had to sleep in at night.

They often went hungry, too. The desert had but little food to give them. They found some edible roots, the sego, and tintic, which is a kind of Indian potato, like the artichoke; they gathered sunflower and balzamoriza [1]

[1] Sometimes called "spring sunflower." It has a blossom much like the sunflower, and velvety leaves. It is common in parts of the West.

seeds, and a few berries. The pitch pine tree gave them pine nuts; and for meat they killed rabbits, prairie dogs, mice, lizards, and even snakes. Once in a great while they got a deer or an antelope. The poor savages had a cold and hungry time of it; we could hardly blame them for stealing our cattle and horses to eat.

Yes, they ate horses, too. That was the reason they had no ponies, as did the Bannocks and Shoshones and other tribes. The Gosiutes wandered afoot over the deserts, but this made them great runners. It is said that Yarabe, one of these Indians, once won a wager by beating the Overland Stage in a race of twenty-five miles

Bur. Am. Ethnology, Smithsonian Institution

Gosiute wickiups in the desert.

over the desert. Swift runners like this would slip in and chase away our animals, driving them off and killing them. Our men finally captured old Umbaginny and some other bad Indians that were making the mischief, and made an example of them.

After this they did not trouble us so much, but the settlements were in constant fear and excitement. One incident connected with my father shows this. Our herd boys were returning from Stansbury Island, in the Great Salt Lake, where many cattle were kept. On their way home they met a band of friendly Indians. The boys, in fun, proposed that the Indians chase them into town, firing a few shots to make it seem like a real attack. The Indians agreed, and the chase began. My father saw them coming and grabbed his gun. Before the white jokers could stop him and explain, he had shot down the head Indian's horse. It took fifty sacks of flour to pay for their fun. The Indians demanded a hundred sacks, but they finally agreed to take half that amount and call things square.

Some of the Indians grew in time to be warm friends with us, and when they did become so, they would help protect us from the wild Indians. At one time Harrison Sevier, a pioneer of Grantsville, was out in the canyon getting wood. " Captain Jack," a chief of the Gosiutes, was with him. Some wild Indians attacked Sevier and would have killed him, but " Captain Jack " sprang to his defense and beat back the murderous Indians. The chief had most of his clothes torn off and was badly bruised in the fight, but he saved his white friend. Not all the Gosiutes were savages. Old Tabby, another of this tribe, was a friend of my father. How he proved his friendship for us I shall tell later.

A rather amusing thing happened one day to Tabby.

He had just got a horse through some kind of trade. Like the other Gosiutes, he was not a very skillful rider. But he would ride his pony. One day this big Indian came galloping along the street towards the blacksmith shop. Riley Judd, the blacksmith, who was always up to pranks, saw Tabby coming, and just as he galloped up, Riley dropped the horse's hoof he was shoeing, threw up his arms and said,

"Why, how dye do, Tabby!"

Tabby's pony jumped sidewise, and his rider tumbled off. He picked himself up and turned to the laughing men, saying —

"Ka wino (no good), Riley Judd, too much how dye do."

Besides our troubles with the Indians, we had to fight the crickets and the grasshoppers. These insects swarmed down from the mountains and devoured every green thing they could find. We had hard work to save our crop. It looked as if starvation was coming. The men got great log rollers and rolled back and forth. Herds of cattle were also driven over the marching crickets to crush them; rushes were piled in their path, and when they crawled into this at night, it would be set on fire. But all seemed in vain. Nothing we could do stopped the scourge.

Then the gulls came by the thousands out of the Great Salt Lake. They dropped among the crickets and gorged and regorged themselves until the foe was checked. No man could pay me money enough to kill one of these birds.

After the cricket war the grasshoppers came to plague us. Great clouds of them would settle down on our fields. Father saved five acres of his grain by giving up the rest to them. We kept the hoppers from settling on this patch by running over and over the field with ropes. We used our bed cords to make a rope long enough.

Dr. *Charles G. Plummer*

Great Salt Lake, Utah, looking south from Bird Island, which is a rookery of hundreds of thousands of gulls, pelicans, and herons. In the distance are Carrington Island (right) and Stansbury Island (left).

But it was a starving winter anyway, in spite of all we could do. We were a thousand miles from civilization, surrounded by hostile Indians. We had very little to eat and next to nothing to wear. It was a time of hunger and hardships; but most of the people managed to live through it, and things grew brighter with the spring.

"He went bucking through the sagebrush."

2   MY LITTLE INDIAN BROTHER

A few tame Indians hung around the settlements begging their living. The people had a saying, "It is cheaper to feed them than to fight them," so they gave them what they could; but the leaders thought it would be better to put them to work to earn their living; so some of the whites hired the Indians. My father made a bargain with old Tosenamp (White-foot) to help him. The Indian had a squaw and one papoose, a boy about my age. They called him Pantsuk.

At that time my father owned a small herd of sheep, and he wanted to move out on his farm, two miles from the settlement, so he could take better care of them. Old Tosenamp thought it would be safe to do so, as most of the Indians there were becoming friendly, and the wild Indians were so far away that it was thought they would not bother us; so we moved out on the farm.

Father put the Indian boy and me to herding the sheep. I had no other boy to play with. Pantsuk and I became greatly attached to each other. I soon learned to talk his language, and Pantsuk and I had great times together for about two years. We trapped chipmunks and birds, shot rabbits with our bows and arrows, and had other kinds of papoose sport.

Once we thought we would have some fun riding the sheep. I caught "Old Carney," our big ram, and Pantsuk got on him; but as his chubby legs were hardly long enough to hold him on the big woolly back, I tied his feet together with a rope under the ram. Old Carney didn't like this. He broke away and went bucking through the sagebrush. Pantsuk tumbled off under him, and the old sheep dragged him for several rods before he got free. Pantsuk was a white papoose for sure, when he scrambled to his feet; but I guess I was more scared than he was. We didn't want any more sheep-back rides.

Some months after this the poor little fellow took sick. We did all we could for him, but he kept getting worse until he died. It was hard for me to part with my dear little Indian friend. I loved him as much as if he had been my own brother.

After Pantsuk died, I had to herd the sheep by myself. The summer·wore along very lonely for me, until about the first of August, when a band of Shoshone Indians came and camped near where I was watching my sheep. Some of them could talk the Gosiute language, which I had learned from my little Indian brother. The Indians seemed to take quite a fancy to me, and they would be with me every chance they could get. They said they liked to hear me talk their language, for they had never heard a white boy talk it as well as I could.

One day an Indian rode up to the place where I was herding. He had with him a little pinto pony. I thought it was the prettiest animal I ever saw. The Indian could talk Gosiute very well. He asked me if I did not want to ride the pony. I told him that I had never ridden a horse. He said that the pony was very gentle, and helped me to mount it. Then he led it around for a while. The next day he came again with the pony and let me ride it. Several other Indians were with him this time. They took turns leading the pony about while I rode it. It was great sport for me. I soon got so I could ride it without their leading it. They kept coming and giving me this fun for several days.

One day, after I had ridden till I was tired, I brought the pony back to the Indian who had first come, and he asked me if I did not want to keep it.

"I would rather have that pony," I replied, "than anything else I ever saw."

"You may have it," he said, "if you will go away with us."

I told him I was afraid to go. He said he would take good care of me and would give me bows and arrows and all the buckskin clothes I needed. I asked him what they had to eat. He said they had all kinds of meat, and berries, and fish, sage chickens, ducks, geese, and rabbits. This sounded good to me. It surely beat living on "lumpy dick" [1] and greens, our usual pioneer fare.

"Our papooses do not have to work," he went on, "they have heap fun all the time, catching fish and hunting and riding ponies."

That looked better to me than herding a bunch of sheep alone in the sagebrush. I told him I would think it over. That night I talked with old Tosenamp. The Indians had tried to get him to help them induce me to go with them. He refused; but he did tell me that they would not hurt me and would treat me all right. The next day I told them I would go.

[1] Made by cooking moistened flour in milk.

My parents knew nothing about it. They would never have consented to my going. And it did look like a foolish, risky thing to do; but I was lonely and tired and hungry for excitement, and I yielded to the temptation. In five days the Indians were to start north to join the rest of their tribe. This Indian was to hide for two days after the rest had gone and then meet me at a bunch of willows about a mile above my father's house after dark with the little pinto pony. The plan was carried out, as you will see. I went with them, and for two years I did not see a white man. This was in August, 1854. I was just about twelve years old at the time.

Shoshone squaws on " pinto " and " buckskin " ponies.

"I jumped on my horse and away we went."

3   OFF WITH THE INDIANS

THE night came at last when we were to leave. Just after dark I slipped away from the house and started for the bunch of willows where I was to meet the Indian. When I got there, I found two Indians waiting for me instead of one. The sight of two of them almost made me weaken and turn back; but I saw with them my little pinto pony and it gave me new courage. They had an old Indian saddle on the pony with very rough rawhide thongs for stirrup straps. At a signal from them, I jumped on my horse and away we went. Our trail led towards the north along the western shore of the Great Salt Lake.

The Indians wanted to ride fast. It was all right at first; but after a while I got very tired. My legs began to hurt me, and I wanted to stop, but they urged me along till the peep of day, when we stopped by some very salt springs. I was so stiff and sore that I could not get off my horse, so one of them lifted me off and stood me on the ground, but I could hardly stand up. The rawhide

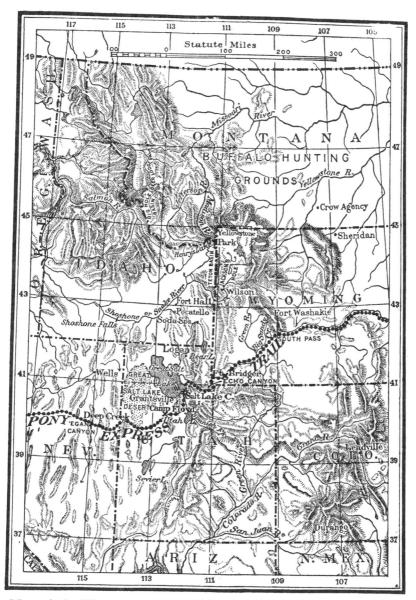

Map of the Western country which was the scene of Uncle Nick's adventures.

straps had rubbed the skin off my legs till they were raw. The Indians told me that if I would take off my trousers and jump into the salt springs it would make my legs better; but I found that I could not get them off alone; they were stuck to my legs. The Indians helped me, and after some very severe pain we succeeded in getting them off. A good deal of skin came with them.

"Come now," they urged me, "jump into this water and you will be well in a little while."

Well, I jumped into the spring up to my waist. Oh blazes! I jumped out again. Oh, my! how it did sting and smart! I jumped and kicked. I was so wild with pain that I lay on the ground and rolled round and round on the grass. After half an hour of this, I wore myself out, and oh, how I cried! The Indians put down a buffalo robe, and rolled me on to it and spread a blanket over me. I lay there and cried myself to sleep.

When I awoke, they were sitting by a small fire. They had killed a duck and were broiling it for breakfast.

"Come," they said, "and eat some duck."

I started to get up, but oh! how sore I was! I began to cry again. They kept coaxing me to come and have something to eat until finally I got up and went to them, but I had to walk on a wide track. I ate some duck and dried meat and felt better. While I was eating they got the horses ready.

"Come," they said, "get on your pony."

"No," I objected, "I can't ride; I'd rather walk."

They said that they were going a long way, and that I could not walk so far. Then they arranged the saddle so it would not hurt me so much, by putting a buffalo robe over it. They lifted me into it. It was not so bad as I thought it would be. The soft hair of the robe made the saddle more comfortable. One of them tied my trousers to my saddle. That day I lost them and for more than two years I did not have another pair. During that time I wore Indian leggings and a blanket.

We traveled all day over a country that was more like the bottom of an old lake than anything else. We camped that night by another spring. The Indians lifted me from my horse, put me down on a robe and started a fire. Then they caught some fish and broiled them again on the coals. It was a fine supper we had that night.

The next morning I felt pretty well used up; but when I had eaten some fish and a big piece of dried elk meat for breakfast, I felt more like traveling. Then we started again.

Near mid-afternoon, we saw, about six miles ahead of us, the Indians we had been trying to overtake. They had joined with another large band, so there were a great many in the camp. By the time we caught up with them, they had stopped and were unpacking, and some of them had their wigwams set up. We rode through the camp until we came to a big tepee where a large, good-looking Indian was standing. This man, they said, was Washakie, their chief; I was to live with him, and he would be my brother.

An old squaw came up to my horse and stood looking at me. The Indians said that she was the chief's mother and that she would be my mother, too. They told her that my legs were badly skinned and were very sore. Then Washakie helped me off my horse.

The old squaw put her hand on my head and began to say something pitiful to me, and I began to cry. She cried, too, and taking me by the arm, led me into the tepee, and pointed to a nice bed the chief's wife had made for me. I lay down on the bed and sobbed myself to sleep. When I awoke, this new mother of mine brought

Bureau of American Ethnology, Smithsonian Institution

Washakie (with hat in hand) and part of his Shoshone tribe at South Pass, Wyoming, in 1861.

me some soup and some fresh deer meat to eat. I tell you it tasted good.

The next morning my new mother thought she would give me a good breakfast. They had brought some flour from the settlements, and she tried to make me some bread, such as I had at home. They had no soda, nothing but flour and water, so the bread turned out to be pretty soggy. I think she didn't like it very well when she found I didn't eat it, but I simply couldn't choke it down. I did make a good meal, however, of the fried sage chicken and the fresh service berries that she brought with the bread.

That day my mother and Hanabi, the chief's wife, started to make me something to wear; for after I lost my trousers, I had nothing but an old thin shirt, out at the elbows, and a straw hat that had lost part of its brim. The two women worked for several hours and finally got the thing finished and gave it to me to put on. I do not know what to call it, for I had never seen anything like it before, but it may have been what the girls now call a "mother-hubbard." It was all right anyhow, when I got it on and my belt around to keep the thing close to me; but I had to pull the back up a little to keep it from choking me to death when I stooped over.

We stayed at this camp for five days to give me time to get well. My good old mother rubbed my legs with skunk oil and they healed rapidly. It had got noised around that my legs were very bad, and one day when I was out in front of the tepee, a lot of papooses wanted to see them. One stooped to raise my mother-hubbard to take a look, and the rest began to laugh, but they didn't laugh long, for I gave him a kick that sent him keeling. Then his mother came out after me, and I thought she was going to eat me up. She scolded and jawed, but I couldn't tell what she was saying, so it did not make much difference to me. My old mother, hearing the noise, came up and led me into the tepee and gave me some dried service berries. I thought that if that was the way they were going to treat me, I would kick another one the first chance I got.

It was not long before I got the chance, for the next day a papoose about my size tried the same trick and I fetched him a kick that made him let out a yell that could have been heard a mile. It brought about half the tribe out to see how many I had killed. That papoose's mother turned loose on me, too, with her tongue and everlastingly berated me. The chief happened to see the trouble, and I think that is what saved me from being cremated. Anyhow, the papooses left my mother-hubbard alone after that.

My mother began then to teach me the Shoshone language. My knowing how to talk the Gosiute tongue made it easier for me, for these two Indian dialects are very much alike.

One night the hunters came in loaded with game, and the next day we began to move. The horses were brought in, and among them was my pinto pony. When I saw him, it seemed like meeting some one from home. I ran up and hugged him. My good old mother had fixed up a pretty good saddle, all cushioned in fine style to keep it from hurting me.

We traveled about fifteen miles that day and camped on a small stream they called Koheets (Curlew). Mother told me to wade out into the water and bathe my legs.

"Not much," I said, "I have had all the baths I want."

She said that the water would make my legs tough, and when she saw I wouldn't go into the stream she brought some cold water and told me to wash them. I wanted to know whether it was salt water. She said it wasn't, so I bathed my legs, and when I found that the water did not hurt them I waded into the creek. Washakie said it was "tibi tsi djant" — heap good.

Dr. T. M. Bridges

Shoshone wickiup. Lodges of this kind were used in the summer season.

4   THE GREAT ENCAMPMENT

IT was the custom of the Shoshone chieftains in those
early days to gather all of their tribe every three years.
As this was the year for the great tribal meeting, we
started for the big camp ground.   After traveling for three
days, we reached a large river, which the Indians called
Piupa (Snake River).   Here we were joined by another
large band of the same tribe.

In order to cross the river, the squaws built boats of
bulrushes tied in bundles ; these bundles were lashed
together until they made a boat big enough to hold up
from six to eight hundred pounds.   The Indians made
the horses swim over, and some of the papoose boys rode
their ponies across.   I wanted to swim my horse, but my
mother would not let me.   It took about a week to get
across the river ; but during that time I had some of the
best fun of my life.

My mother gave me a fishhook and a line made out of
hair from a horse's tail.   With this tackle I caught my

first fish, and some of them were very large ones, too. The other boys became more friendly, and we had jolly times together; but mother kept pretty close watch over me, for fear I would kick them, and get into more trouble. After I began to play with the papooses, I picked up the Shoshone language much faster.

Nothing else of importance happened until we reached Big Hole Basin. There I saw the first buffalo I had seen since crossing the plains. Seven head of them appeared one morning on a hill about a mile away. Ten Indians started after them. One, having a wide, blade-like spear-head attached to a long shaft, would ride up to a buffalo and cut the hamstrings of both legs, then the others would rush up and kill the wounded animal.

About fifteen squaws followed the hunters to skin the buffaloes and get the meat. Mother and I went with them. The squaws would rip the animals down the back from head to tail, then rip them down the belly and take off the top half of the hide and cut away all the meat on that side from the bones. They would tie ropes to the feet of the carcass and turn it over with their ponies, to strip off the skin and flesh from the other side in the same way.

The meat was then carried to camp to be

Meat drying before the tepee of a Crow Indian.

J. E. *Stimson*

Snake River (Piupa), in the land of the Snoshones.

sliced in thin strips and hung up to dry. When it was about half dry, the squaws would take a piece at a time and pound it between two stones till it was very tender. It was then hung up again to dry thoroughly. The dried meat was put into a sack and kept for use in the winter and during the general gatherings of the tribe. The older it got the better it was. This is the way the Indians cured all of their buffalo meat. Washakie had about five hundred pounds of such meat for his own family when we reached Deer Lodge Valley, now in Montana, the place of our great encampment.

It was about the last of August before all of the tribe had assembled. What a sight it was to see so many Indians together! The tepees were strung up and down the stream as far as I could see, and the whole country round about was covered with horses and dogs. As nearly as I could find out, about six thousand Indians had gathered. When I asked the chief how many there were, he said that he could not count them. And to think that I was the only white person within hundreds of miles, perhaps! It gave me rather a queer feeling.

Mother kept very close watch over me for fear that I should get hurt or lost among so many Indians. Whenever I went around to see what was going on, she was nearly always by my side. She warned me especially against Pocatello's Indians, telling me that they were very bad, that they would steal me and take me away off and sell me to Indians that would eat me up. She scared me so badly that I stuck pretty close to her most of the time.

The Indians spent much of their time horse-racing and gambling. They would bet very heavily; I saw an Indian win fifty head of ponies on one race. Two Indians were killed while racing their horses, and a squaw

Shoshone Indians dancing.

and her papoose were run over; the papoose was also killed.

Some of Pocatello's Indians had several scalps they had taken from some poor emigrants they had killed. I saw six of these scalps. One was of a woman with red hair, one a girl's scalp with dark hair, and four were men's scalps, one with gray hair, the rest with dark hair. I cannot describe the feelings I had when I saw the red devils dancing around those scalps. It made me wish that I were home again herding sheep and living on "lumpy dick" and greens.

Washakie's Indians had a few Crow scalps, for at this time the Shoshones and Crows were at war with each other. I am pretty sure that they had no white scalps; or if they had, they did not let me see them.

The Indians had great times dancing around the scalps. They would stick a small pole in the ground and string scalps on it. Then they would dance around it, singing and yelling at the top of their voices, making the most horrible noises I ever heard. The leaders of the different bands would take the inside, the warriors would circle about them and the squaws and papooses would dance around the outside. The noise they made would shame a band of coyotes. As many as five hundred Indians would be dancing in this way at one time, and they would keep at it for hours. I got sick and tired of their hideous noises; but they thought they were having a high time. This singing and dancing was kept going at intervals for a week or more.

The time was drawing near when we were to separate, and I was glad of it. Some of Pocatello's Indians left a few days ahead of the rest of his band. A day or two before our band was to start my pinto pony ran off with some other horses. I slipped away from my mother and went after him. Before I had gone far I met some Indians hunting horses, but they said they had not seen mine. I kept on going until another Indian came up to me. He said he had seen some horses go over a ridge about a mile away.

"If you will get on my horse behind me," he said, "I will take you over and see if your horse is there." Thinking no harm, I got on his horse and off we started; but when we got to the top of the hill no horses were to be seen. After we got over the hill he began to ride fast. I got scared, for I thought of the man-eating savages my mother had told me about. I asked him to stop and let me get off, but he only whipped his horse harder and went faster.

Watching my chance, I jumped off and almost broke my neck; but I got up and put back towards camp as hard as I could run. The Indian turned, dashed up, and threw his lasso over me. After dragging me several rods he stopped, and hit me with his quirt, telling me to get back on his horse or he would put an arrow through me. I cried and begged him to let me go; but he made me get on again, and then he struck off as fast as he could go. I noticed, however, that he kept looking back every little while.

Pretty soon he stopped and told me to get off. As I jumped he gave me a lick over the head with his quirt that made me see stars for a few minutes. Then he started off on the run again; but after going about fifty yards he stopped, pulled his bow and arrow out of his quiver and started towards me as if he intended to put an arrow through me. He came but a few steps, then suddenly whirled his horse and off he went over the prairie.

I soon saw what caused his hurry. A short distance

away were some Indians coming towards me as fast as they could travel. When they reached me, they stopped, and one of them told me to get on behind him and he would take me to my mother. I climbed up double quick. Before we got to the tepees I met mother coming out to find me. She was crying. She took me off the horse and threw her arms around me. One of Pocatello's Indians, she said, was trying to steal me and she never expected to find her white papoose again.

Some Indians happened to see me get on my horse behind the Indian and told my mother, and Washakie had sent those Indians after me, before we got very far away. Mother stayed close to me after that; but I had had such a scare that I didn't go very far from the tepee without her. The chief told me never to go alone after my horse if he got away again, but to let him know and he would have the pony brought back. "If Pocatello's Indians," he said, "could get you, they would swap you for a whole herd of ponies, and then it would be 'good-by Yagaiki.'" "Yagaiki," by the way, was my Indian name. It meant "the crier." They gave it to me because I mimicked the squaws and papooses one day when they were bawling about something.

5   BREAKING CAMP

THE camp finally began to break up in earnest. Small bands went off in different directions to their various hunting grounds that had been decided on by the council. We were among the last to leave. There were about sixty tepees and two hundred and fifty Indians in our band. We had about four hundred horses, and more than five hundred dogs, it seemed to me.

Chief Washakie at that time was about twenty-seven years old. He was a very large Indian and good looking. His wife, Hanabi, did not appear to be more than twenty years old. She had only one child, a little boy papoose about six months old.

Pocatello was not so large as Washakie. He was a Shoshone, but his wife was a Bannock. She had three papooses when I first saw her. Pocatello was a wicked looking Indian. His tribe did more damage to the emigrants than any other tribe in the West. He wanted to be the big chief of the Shoshones; he thought he ought to be the leader because he was older than Washakie, but the tribe would not have it that way. He did draw away about five hundred of the tribe, however, and tried to change the tribe name to "Osasibi"; but Washakie's Indians called them "Saididig," which means dog-stealers.

When this band of Indian outlaws joined us in the Big Hole Basin, they had new quilts, white women's clothes, new guns, watches, saddles, and hats. Mother told me that they had just attacked a large train of emigrants, and had killed the people, burned their wagons and robbed them of everything. They had some very large horses and mules with them. Mother wanted to buy a saddle and a hat for me, but I told her that I would not wear a hat whose owner had been killed and scalped by old Pocatello.

Washakie and Pocatello were never very friendly. Pocatello wanted to keep up a constant warfare against the whites; but Washakie knew that meant only trouble and that the Indians would finally get the worst of it; so he would have nothing to do with Pocatello's murderous business. Because Washakie thought it would be much better to live in peace with the whites, Pocatello called him a squaw and said he was afraid to fight.

I was very glad to go; for I was tired of being stared at by so many Indians. There were hundreds of young Indians in the camp and many old ones, too, that had never seen a white person before. They would gather around me as if I were some wild animal. If I moved more suddenly towards them, they would jump back and scream like wildcats. My mother told them that I would not bite, but if they bothered me too much I might kick some of their ribs loose, for I could kick worse than a wild horse.

Two or three days after we had left the big camp, the

L. A. *Huffman, Miles City, Mont.*
Buffaloes on the plains.

pack on one of our horses turned under his belly and he began to run and kick like mad. This started the rest of the pack horses and they came running past us. Mother tried to stop them, but one of the runaways bumped against her horse and knocked it down. It rolled over with her. I thought she was killed. I jumped from my horse and raised her up. She was not dead, but she was badly bruised and one of her arms was broken. I think I never cried harder in my life than I did then, for I thought my poor mother was going to die. She told me not to cry, that she would be all right soon.

Washakie's wife was there and she told me to dash ahead and tell the chief to hurry back. When he came, he ordered the band to stop and pitch camp. We had to stay there a week to let mother get well enough to travel again. There were a great many antelope in the valley and plenty of fish in the stream by the camp. When mother would go to sleep, I would go fishing. When she awoke Hanabi would call, "Yagaiki come," and I would get back in double-quick time.

One day while we were camped here waiting for mother to get better, I went out with Washakie and the other Indians to chase antelope. About fifty of us circled around a bunch and took turns chasing them. The poor little animals were gradually worn out by this running and finally they would drop down one after another, hiding their heads under the bushes, while the Indians shot them to death with their bows and arrows. I killed two myself. When I got home and told mother about it, she bragged about me so much that I thought I was a "heap big Injun."

Mother's arm soon got well enough for her to travel, for the medicine man had fixed it up very well, so we took up our journey again. There were a great many buffaloes and antelope too, where we next pitched camp. We stayed there for about three weeks. During the times that she could not watch me, mother had Washakie take me out on his hunting trips. That just suited me. It was lots of fun to watch the Indian with the big spear dash up and cut the hamstrings of the great animals. When they had been crippled in this way, we would rush up and shoot arrows into their necks until they dropped dead. The first day we killed six, two large bulls and four cows.

L. A. Huffman, Miles City, Mont.

Why the buffalo disappeared; part of the white man's trail.

I told Washakie that my bow was too small to kill buffaloes with. He laughed and said I should have a bigger one. When we got back to camp, he told some Indians what I had said and one very old Indian, whose name was Morogonai, gave me a very fine bow and another Indian gave me eight good arrows. I felt very proud then; I told mother that the next time I went out I would kill a whole herd of buffaloes. She said she knew I would, but she did not know what they could do with all the meat.

Washakie said that I was just like the rest of the white men. They would kill buffaloes as long as there were any in sight and leave their carcasses over the prairies for the wolves. He said that was not the way of the Indians. They killed only what they needed and saved all the meat and hides.

"The Great Spirit," he said, "would not like it if we slaughtered the game as the whites do. It would bring bad luck, and the Indians would go hungry if they killed the deer and buffaloes when they were not needed for food and clothing."

Two or three days after this we went out again and killed two more buffaloes. When we got back mother asked how many I had killed. I told her that I shot twice at them and I believed I had hit one. She said that I would be the best hunter in the tribe afterwhile, and some day, she said, I would be a big chief.

6　VILLAGE LIFE

COLD weather was coming. Some snow had already fallen
in the mountains. Hanabi and her friends went to work
to make me some better clothes. Very soon they had a
fine suit ready.

The trousers part was made somewhat like the chaps
worn by cowboys, being open in front, with no seat; but
on the sides they had wedge-shaped strips that ran up and
fastened to the belt. These leggings fitted pretty tight, but
there was a seam about as wide as my hand that could be
let out if necessary. They gave me a pair of new moccasins that came up to my knees. They also made me another overshirt, or "mother-hubbard," out of fine smoked
buckskin; it fitted me better than did my first one. The
sleeves came down a little below my elbows and had a
long fringe from the shoulders down; it was also fringed
around the neck and the bottom ; and to touch it up more,
they had stitched beads in heart and diamond shapes
over the breast. The clothes were all very fine ; but when
I got them on, I looked a good deal like a squaw papoose.

Lee Moorhouse

Indian camp by a river.

I didn't care much, though, for the clothes fitted me pretty well and they were warm and comfortable. Mother also made me a hat out of muskrat skin. It ran to a peak and had two rabbit tails sewed to the top for tassels. With my new clothes on, I was better dressed than any other kid in camp.

We now started for the elk country. When we got there, the Indians killed about one hundred elk and a few bear; but by that time it was getting so cold that we set out for our winter quarters. After traveling a few days we reached a large river, called by the Indians Piatapa, by the whites the Jefferson River; it is now in Montana. Here we pitched camp to stay during the "snowy moons."

Most of the buffaloes by this time had left for their winter range; but once in a while we saw a few as they passed our camp. The Indians did not bother them, however, because we had plenty of dried meat, and for fresh meat there were many white-tail deer that we could snare by hanging loops of rawhide over their trails through the willows. There were also a great many grouse and sage hens about in the brush. I have killed as many as six or seven of these a day with my bow and arrows.

Winter passed away very slowly. Nothing exciting happened until along towards spring; then one day we had a terrible fracas. Washakie had gone up the river a few miles to visit another large Indian village for a day or two. While he was away, pretty nearly all the camp got into a fight.

We had a fishing hole close to camp where the squaws and papooses would fish. Mother and I had been down there with the others fishing through this hole in the ice, and when we had caught a good string of fish mother took what we had to the tepee. She told me not to stay long.

As soon as she had gone, a girl, a little larger than I, wanted to take my tackle and fish in my hole. I let her have it, and she caught several fish. Then I heard mother call me and I asked the girl to give me back my pole so I could go home, but she would not do it. I tried to take it from her, but she jerked it away and hit me over the head with it, knocking me to my knees. I jumped up and gave her a whack that knocked her down; when she got up she let out some of the awfulest yelps I ever heard. Then she put for home as fast as she could go, yelling and screaming. I knew something else would happen pretty quick; so I gathered up what fish the other papooses hadn't run away with and hiked for home too. Just as I got inside the tepee, the girl's mother came rushing up with a big knife in her hand. "Give me that little white devil!" she screamed. "I'll cut his heart out!" She started for me, but mother stopped her, and shoved her back out of the tepee.

They made such a racket that the whole camp gathered around to see the fun. The squaw hit mother over the head with the knife; and when I saw the blood fly, I grabbed a stick and struck the squaw over the head, knocking her down. Another squaw grabbed mother and I sent her spinning. Then others mixed in and took sides and soon the whole bunch was yelling and fighting fit to kill. One boy grabbed my stick, but I gave him a kick that settled him. Then Hanabi took the stick from me: but I ran into the tepee and grabbed my bow and arrows. I was so mad I would have made a few "good squaws" in quick time; but a big Indian jerked my bow from me and broke the string. I guess it was best that he did. More Indians rushed up and stopped the fight; but not before a lot of them went off howling with sore heads. That night Washakie came home and held a big council.

I don't know what they said, but the next day two or three families left our camp and went to join another band.

Everything now passed along very well for a time. I helped mother carry wood and water. The boy papooses made fun of me, calling me a squaw for doing it, because carrying wood and water was squaw's work. I told mother that I would break some of their necks

The seed gatherers of Western desert tribes.

if they didn't stop it. "Oh, let them alone," she said, "they are bad boys."

But one day we were getting wood, and having cut more than we could carry in one trip, I went back for it when a boy ran up to me and said, "You're a squaw," and spit at me. I threw down my wood and struck out after him. He ran yelping at every jump, expecting me, I guess, to kick his head off. But Washakie happened to see us and called to me to stop. It was lucky for that papoose that he did. I went back and got my wood and took it to the tepee.

Washakie wanted to know what it was all about. I told him what the boy had done. He said he did not want to start another camp fight, but he did want me to take my own part. He said that he had been watching how things were going, and he was glad to say that, so far as he knew, I had never started a fuss. He did not think that I was quarrelsome if I was let alone. He was glad, he said, to see me stand up for myself; for if I was cowardly the papooses would give me no peace.

One day I heard an Indian talking to Washakie and telling him it was not right for him to let me do squaw's work; it would set a bad example for the other boys. Washakie replied that he thought it was a good example, and if some of the older ones would take it, it would be better for their squaws.

"We burden our women to death," he said, "with hard labor. I did not think so much about it until Yagaki came. I see now how much he helps mother and how much hard work she has to do. Yagaki appears to be happier helping mother than he is when playing with the other boys. I believe that she would have gone crazy if it had not been for him, her troubles over the loss of father and my brothers were so great. I do believe that the Great Spirit sent the little white boy to her."

I think myself that if anything had happened to me, it would have killed mother. She was very proud to have me with her. She would say to Washakie, "Yagaki is a smart boy. He asks me questions that I can hardly answer. One day he asked me why the Indians did not haul and cut the wood for their women. His father does that for his mother. He thinks that the Indians ought to pack the meat, too, and take care of their own horses, or send the boys to do it. If the women tanned the hides and made the moccasins and clothes for the family and did the cooking, it was their share of the work."

I heard all this talk going on one night when they thought I was asleep. Washakie agreed with most of what his mother said, but of course they couldn't change the Indians' way of doing things.

"She used to tell me her troubles."

7 MY INDIAN MOTHER

My Indian mother was as good and kind to me as any one could be, but she did not seem to realize that there was another loving mother miles and miles away whose heart was sorrowing because of my absence. To her mind must have come many times these words of the old song: "Oh, where is my wandering boy tonight?"

My Indian mother would often ask me a good many questions about my white mother. She asked me if I did not want to go home. I told her that I should like to see my folks very much, but if I went home they would keep me there, and I did not want to herd sheep. I told her that I would rather play with white boys than with Indian boys, but that I liked my bow and arrows, and father would not let me have these at home because I would be shooting at the cats and chickens all the time. "I like my pony too, and I could not take him home," I said, "and I love you too. If I went away you could not go with me; so taking it all around I should rather stay with you."

This always seemed to please her; for her face would light up and sometimes a tear would steal down her brown cheeks, and then she would grab me and hug me until you could hear my ribs crack.

Often she would tell me about her troubles. Her husband had been shot a few years before in the knee with a poisoned arrow by the Crow Indians. He lived a little over a year after the battle, but he suffered greatly before he died. Soon after his death her two boys named Piubi and Yaibi went out hunting mountain sheep. While they were climbing a steep hill, a snowslide crashed down and buried them in the deep gorge at the bottom of the canyon. Here they lay until late in the following spring. The Indians tried to find their bodies by pushing long sticks into the snow, but they could not locate them.

But their mother would not give up the search. She told me how she would go out every day and dig in the snow with a stick in the hope of finding her boys, until she got so sick that Washakie and some other Indians brought her home, where she lay for two months very near death from sorrow and exposure.

As soon as she could walk she went up to the snowslide again. The warmer weather by this time had melted some of the snow, and she found the body of one of her boys partly uncovered. The wolves had eaten off one of his feet. She quickly dug the body out of the snow, and near by she found the other boy. She was too weak to carry them back to the tepee, and she couldn't leave them there to be eaten by the wolves, so she stayed all night watching over them.

The next morning Washakie found her lying on the snow beside the bodies of her children. He took them up tenderly and carried them back to the village. The poor old mother was very sick after that. During this sickness and delirium of grief, she dreamed that her youngest boy came back to her, and he was white. This dream put into her mind the strange notion that she wanted a white papoose.

She was just getting well when the band of Indians she was with came into the settlement where I lived and found me. When they found that I could talk the Indian tongue, they decided that I was just the boy for the chief's mother. They asked Washakie about it. He would not let them steal me, but he said that if they could lure me away from home, it was all right with him. So they set to work, as I have told, and succeeded in tempting me to go away with them.

My old mother also told me many things that happened when she was a little girl. She said that her father was a Shoshone, and her mother a Bannock. She said she was sixty-two "snows" (years) old when I came. She had had four children, three boys and a girl. When the girl was seven years old, she was dragged to death by a horse. Her two sons were killed by the snowslide, so Washakie and I were the only ones she had left.

Her life, she said, had been filled with sorrow, but she was having better times now than she had ever had before. If I would stay with her, she would be happy once more. She said she had fifteen head of horses of her own. When she died she wanted Washakie and me to divide them between us. She also wanted me, when she died, to bury her as the white folks bury their dead, as she thought that way was the best.

She certainly was good to me, watching me night and day and doing everything she could for my comfort, and I tried to be good and kind to her in return, but sometimes, boylike, I forgot. One night I was playing with the Indian boys. Our game was killing white men. With

42

J. E. Stimson

Death's Canyon, Teton Range, Jackson's Hole, Wyoming; snow slide
in ravine at left.

our bows and arrows, we would slip up to the bunches of brush and shoot at them. If we clipped off a twig with the arrow, that was a scalp. We would stick it in our belts and strut about like big Injuns.

While our fun was on, I heard mother call, "Yagaki, come in and go to bed." I paid no attention so she came out and said, "Why didn't you come when I called you?" "I didn't want to go to bed," I answered sulkily. With that she grabbed me by the collar and jerked me toward the tepee. I begged and promised, but she kept me going till she got me inside; then she flung me down on a pile of blankets.

"Washakie," she said, "you must do something with this boy. He won't mind me." With that she left the tent and I heard her crying outside.

The chief looked at me a minute, then he said quietly: "What is the trouble between you and mother?"

"Well, she won't let me play," I said; "she makes me come in every night before dark. The other boys stay out; I don't see why I can't."

"Mother knows why," he said. "You should be good to her and mind her; she is good to you — better than she ever was to me."

Mother had come in again. "Yagaki," she said, "you must not stay out after dark. Those papooses might kill you. They have been trained to think it is an honor to kill a white man. If they could do it without being seen, they would just as soon put an arrow through you as not. I know what is best for you, Yagaki. You must come when I call."

I always obeyed her after that, and we got along very well. She was a dear old mother to me.

8   THE CROWS

As winter began to break up we got ready to move to the spring hunting grounds, but when we rounded up our horses we found that about fifty head of the best ones were missing. The Crow Indians had stolen them. Our Indians found their trail and followed them, but the Crows had so much the start that our braves could not overtake them.   We never recovered our animals. Among the lost horses were six that belonged to mother and eleven of Washakie's horses.   My little pinto was not missing, for I had kept him close to camp with the horses we had used during the winter.

Our Indians were angry.   They declared that they would get even with the Crows before another winter had passed.   And I suppose they did it, for the two tribes were constantly stealing from each other.   The Crows would steal every horse they could from the Shoshones;   and our Indians would do the same with them.   It was as fair for one tribe as it was for the other.   They would fight, too, every time they met.   Each tribe was always on the watch to get the advantage over the other; so we were in a constant state of excitement, and war dances were going on all the time.

When we left our winter camp, we started south. After two days' travel, we joined another large Indian camp, and kept with them during our wanderings the rest of the summer.

For three or four more days we all traveled south again. The game was plentiful here, elk, deer, antelope, and buffalo, so we camped for several days and stocked up with fresh meat. Then we took up the trail again, this time going east till we came to a beautiful lake that was fairly alive with fish. Oh, how I did catch them!

It was a great game country, too. We could see buffaloes at any time and in any direction that we looked. There were herds of antelope over the flats. I had great fun running them. Washakie said that I was riding my horse too much, that he was getting thin. He told me to turn the pony out, and he would give me another horse. I was very glad to let my little pinto have a rest and get fat again.

The horse that Washakie gave me was a pretty roan, three years old, and partly broken. When the chief saw how well I managed my new horse, he said that I might break some other young horses for him to pay for the roan. That just suited me, for I liked the excitement of training wild horses. The Indian ponies were small, especially the colts that he wanted broken. I wanted to get right at it, but he said that I must wait till they got fat, so that they could buck harder.

At this time we were not far from the Crow country. There was a dispute between the tribes about the boundary line that divided our hunting grounds from theirs. One day some of our hunters came rushing to camp badly

American Museum of Natural History

Elk in their mountain home.

scared. They said that the Crows were right on us. I never saw such excitement in my life. Everybody in camp was running about and talking excitedly. The bucks were getting ready to fight ; the horses were rounded up and driven into camp. It was a great mixup — horses, squaws, dogs, papooses, tepees, and bucks all jumbled together.

The War Chief ordered the young warriors to go out and meet the Crows. The old men were left to guard camp. I started to get my horse.

"If I am going to fight," I said, "I want my pinto pony."

Mother stopped me, "Here, you little dunce," she said, "you are not going to fight. You couldn't fight anything. I don't believe there is going to be a fight anyway. I have had too many such Crow scares."

I wondered whether the Crows had wings like the crows in our country. She said that they were Indians like the Shoshones.

By this time the squaws had everything packed and

A Crow encampment (Crow Agency, Montana).

ready to fling on to the horses that were standing about with their saddles on. The old bucks were gathered in small groups here and there talking all at the same time. But the excitement soon passed over; for the warriors came back after a little while to tell us that it was not Crows at all but a herd of buffaloes that had caused the scare. I was rather disappointed, for I wanted to see some fun. I began to think that they were cowards — the whole bunch of them. But they were not. The next day a band of about fifty young warriors left for some place. I could not find out where they were going, but they seemed to mean business.

For a while after this scare everything passed off peacefully. We fished and chased antelope, and one day I went with Washakie up into the mountains to kill elk. We had not gone far till we saw a large herd of these animals lying down. Leaving our horses, we crept up close to them. Washakie had a good gun, and at his first shot he hit a big cow elk. She ran about a minute before she fell. The chief told me to slip up and shoot her in the neck with my arrows till she was dead, then to cut her throat so that she would bleed freely; and to stay there till he came back. Well, I crept up as close as I dared, and shot every arrow I had at her. Then I climbed a tree. I guess she was dead before I shot her, but I was not sure, for I was afraid to go up near enough to see. Washakie followed the herd that ran down the canyon.

I stayed up the tree for some time, then came down quietly and went up to the elk and threw sticks at her, but she did not move, so I plucked up courage and cut her throat. She had been dead so long that she did not bleed a bit.

I waited and waited for Washakie to come back. After a while I began to get scared. I thought that the bears would smell the elk and finding me there would eat me up, so I put off to where we had left our horses; but I could not find them. Then I started back to the elk, but I could not find it. I was so bewildered that I did not know what to do. The timber was thick, and I was getting more scared all the time. I tried again to find our horses and failed. By this time the sun had gone down, and it was very gloomy among the trees. I climbed another tree and waited for a long

A Crow Indian tepee.

time. I was afraid to call for fear of bringing a bear on to me.

Afterwards, I learned that I had not left the elk long before Washakie came and took the entrails out of it, and as he did not see my horse, he thought that I had gone to camp. Before following the elk, he had tied my horse to a tree, but it had broken loose and run away. When Washakie reached camp, some Indians told him that they had seen my horse loose with the saddle on. He did not know what to do. Mother was frantic. She started right out to hunt me, and a big band of Indians followed her.

A little while after dark I heard the strange noise they were making. I thought the Crows were after me; so I

kept quiet, but pretty soon I heard some one calling —
"Yagaki! Yagaki!" Then I knew that it was one of
our Indians, so I answered him. In a little while there
was a crackling of brush right under my tree.

"Where were you?" he shouted.

"Here I am," I said.

"What were you doing up there?" he asked.

"Looking for my horse."

"Well, you won't find him up there," he said. "Come
down here."

I minded him in a hurry.

"Now, get on behind me," he said; "the whole tribe
is looking for you, and your poor mother is nearly crazy
about you. It would be better for her if some one would
kill you, and I have a notion to do it. It would save her
lots of trouble."

When he got out of the timber, he began to halloo just
as loud as he could to let the rest know that I was found.
Then I could hear the Indians yelling all through the
woods. We reached camp before mother came in, and I
wanted to go back to look for her, but Hanabi would not
let me. She said that I might get lost again; that I had
given mother trouble enough for one night.

It was not long before mother came. She grabbed me
in her arms and said, "Yagaki, Yagaki, where have you
been? I was afraid a bear had eaten you." She talked
and cried for almost an hour. She blamed Washakie for
leaving me alone and said that I should never go off with
him again; she would keep me close to her.

The next morning I went with mother and another
squaw to get the elk. Washakie asked me if I thought
I could find it. I told him that I knew I could, so we
started and I led them right to it. As we were skinning
the elk, mother said that I had spoiled the skin by

shooting it so full of holes. But the meat was fat and tender.

About ten days after this our band of young warriors came back. They had captured thirty-two head of horses, but one of our Indians had been killed in the skirmish they had with the Crows. One of the band told me all about their raid. He said that they went over to the headwaters of the Missouri River — Sogwobipa, the Indians called it. There they found a small band of Crow Indians, but the Crows had seen them first, and were ready for them. Just after dark our Indians tried to run off a band of Crow horses they had seen, but they were met with a shower of arrows and a few bullets which killed one of their party and wounded five or six of their horses. One horse was so badly crippled that he could not travel, so the rider jumped on to the horse belonging to the dead Indian and they all broke back as fast as their horses could carry them. They were chased by the Crows all night, but they finally made their escape.

A few days after this as they were going through a range of mountains, they came suddenly upon a small band of Crows, killed two of them and took all their horses. They thought the whole tribe of Crows was following them, so they made a bee line for home. I thought it was pretty rough for about fifty to jump on a few like that, kill some and rob the rest of their horses. I think that Washakie did not like it either. When I told him that it was not fair, he said it was too bad, but that the Crows would have treated us just the same.

The Indians were uneasy. They felt sure that the Crows would follow and attack us any minute, so we kept a strong guard out all the time. Washakie thought it best to get a little farther from the border line and in a more open country where they could watch the horses

52

Albert Schlechten, Bozeman, Mont.

Headwaters of Missouri River. Montana. The Gallatin, Jefferson, and Madison rivers join here to make the Missouri River. The country around these rivers was a great hunting ground in the early days for Shoshones, Crows, Nez Percé, Selish, and other Indian tribes.

better. The Indians did not appear to value their own lives so much as they did their horses.

I asked Washakie why it would not be better for the chiefs to get together, talk the matter over, and stop this stealing and fighting. He laughed and said that when I got older I might fix things to suit myself, but as things were going there, he had to be a little careful. Some of his men would rather be fighting than at peace; and Pocatello was poisoning the minds of as many of the tribe as he could with the spirit of war, to draw them away with him. For his part, Washakie said, he would rather live at peace.

The camp packed up and made a start from the open country. We made a long string of Indians, horses, and dogs trailing through the hills. For about a week we kept traveling southward along the river that came out of the beautiful lake until we reached another large stream. When these two streams came together, they made a very large river. It was the Piupa, or Snake River, which we had crossed before. We pitched our tepees by a stream that flowed into the north fork of this big river. It was not very wide, but it was deep and full of fish. We papooses had heaps of fun catching them.

After we had been in camp here a few days, Washakie told me that I might begin breaking the colts. That was more fun for me. We caught one, tied it to a tree and let it stand there until it stopped pulling back, then we led it to water. We staked it out near camp and let it stay there to feed all night. The next morning I found that I could lead it alone to water, so I thought I would try to ride it.

I was putting my saddle on it when mother said, "You had better ride it bareback." I told her that I could not stay on without my saddle, so she told me to do as I liked.

The colt, however, objected so strongly to being saddled that he came near getting away from me.

"Put a blanket over its head, so it cannot see," said mother.

I tied the broncho to a brush, threw a blanket over its head, and mother helped me to tie it on. By this time about fifty kids had gathered around to see the fun. When the saddle was cinched, mother said, "Now get on and I will pull the blanket off its head."

I mounted carefully and then said, "Let him go." Off came the blanket and away went the horse. He whirled and sprang into the air, coming down with his head between his forelegs. I went flying toward the creek, and I didn't stop till I got to the bottom of it. When I crawled out and wiped the water out of my eyes, I could see that colt going across the prairie with my saddle under his belly and kicking at every jump.

"Let him go," said my mother, as I started after him.

I said I would ride that horse if I never killed another Indian.

"How many have you killed?" she asked in surprise.

"Not half as many as I am going to," I said. "And I have half a notion to start in on some of these black imps that are laughing at me."

When I got some dry clothes on, a young Indian rode up on a horse and I got him to go and catch the colt for me. He brought the broncho back and helped me tie a strap around him so tight I could just put my fingers under it, then he held the colt while I got on him.

When I said, "Let him go!" the colt leaped into a run and the young Indian followed after me, keeping it out of the brush and away from the horses that were staked around. The colt soon got tired and stopped running. I had a fine ride. After a while we went back to camp and I staked the colt out for the night. The next day I rode the broncho again, and very soon I had it well trained.

It took mother and me some time to gather up my saddle, and when we got it together we could hardly tell what it had been in the first place; but after about a week of mending, we made it a great deal stouter than it was. The next colt was not so fractious and I soon got so that I could ride any of them without much trouble.

About this time we had another stampede. One night a guard came running into camp with the word that he had seen a big band of Crows coming. It was in the middle of the night, but all of the squaws and papooses were pulled out of bed and ordered to get into the brush and stay there till morning. I told mother that I would not go one step without my horse. She said that I could not find him in the dark, but I was certain that I knew right where he was, and off I put with mother after me calling, "Yagaki, Yagaki, come back, come back." I outran her, however, and happened to find my pinto. Jumping on it I dashed back to mother. She scolded me and told me that the Crows might have got me; but I said I would have to see the Crows before I believed there were any within a hundred miles of us.

The Indians, however, gathered up all their horses and stayed around them all night. Mother, Hanabi, and I went down to the river about a mile away to hide among the willows and trees with seven or eight hundred other squaws and papooses. They made such a racket with their excited talking and crying that no one could sleep. All of them expected to be killed before morning.

But morning came and no Crows. The Indians were mad as hornets, or at least they acted that way. Washakie sent out some men to where the guard said he saw the Crows. They found that he had seen only a big dust and thought it was made by their enemies. I asked Washakie if he thought that there was any real danger of the Crows coming to attack us. He said that he did not think they would come to fight us in this place, but that they might try to steal our horses, or even attack small bands of our Indians if they ran on to them away from camp.

Every once in a while after that we would have a Crow scare. If the Indians saw a cloud of dust, they thought the Crows were after them. They acted like a band of sheep that had been run by coyotes. Every little thing would scare them. It made me tired to see them so cowardly. I told Washakie that I did not think they would fight if they had a chance.

"When are you going to send more Indians out to steal the Crows' horses?" I asked him.

"Why, do you want to go with them?"

I told him that I had not lost any horses.

"Well, we have," he said, "and we are going to get them back before snow flies. The War Chief will attend to that."

I found out afterwards that Washakie meant business. He was no coward.

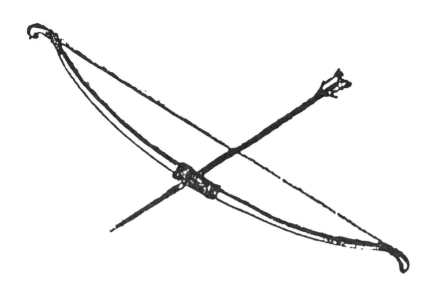

9 PAPOOSE TROUBLES

AFTER this second Crow scare, things quieted down again. I kept on breaking colts, and whipping kids once in a while. One day while I was riding a wild colt, the boy whom I had kicked before for trying to see my sore legs began to act smart again. He was riding with other papooses along with me to see the fun, and every once in a while he would poke my pony with a stick to see him jump. I warned him once or twice to quit; but this only seemed to make him worse.

I had a long rawhide rope around the colt's neck, and I made a noose in the loose end. When he punched my horse again, I flung the lasso over his head and jerked him from his pony. This scared my broncho and he broke into a run. Before I could stop him, I had nearly choked the life out of that kid. The blood was coming out of his nose and mouth and I thought that I had surely killed him; but as soon as I loosened the rope, he began to bawl, and when he got up he put out for camp on the dead run, yelling and groaning as if he was being murdered.

I started for camp, too, for I knew that things would be popping pretty soon. As he passed our camp, mother asked who had hurt him. "Yagaki!" he cried, running on to his mother.

Before I got home, mother met me and asked, "What have you been doing, Yagaki?"

"Trying to kill that blamed kid," I said.

"Well, you have nearly done it this time," she said. "How did it happen?"

I told her all about it.

"It will cause another camp fight," she said.

I turned loose the colt I was riding and started after my pinto pony.

"Where are you going?" she asked me.

"After my horse."

"What for?"

"Because I want him."

When I had caught and saddled my pony I saw the boy and his father and mother with some more Indians coming towards our tent. I jumped on my horse and started off. Mother called to me to stop, but I kept on going. I thought that if they wanted to fight they could fight; I was going to get out of it as fast as my pinto could carry me, so I went up the river and hid in the brush. After dark I heard the Indians calling "Yagaki, Yagaki," but I would not answer them.

After a while the mosquitoes got so bad in the brush that I could not stay there, so when everything was still I crept out, but I did not know where to go or what to do. I sat down on a stump and tried to decide. I knew that there would be a racket in camp and I felt bad on account of mother, but I was not a bit sorry for the papoose I had hurt; just then I almost wished I had killed him. I had some pretty mean feelings as I sat there on the

Bur. Am. Ethnology, Smithsonian Institution
Indian girls carrying water.

stump. I was more homesick than I had ever been before.

It was not a very pleasant situation, I tell you, to be so far away from home among a lot of Indians who were mad at me. I did not know but that they would kill me. I was worried; but after thinking the matter over I decided that it would be better for me to go back and face the music.

When I got near camp I met a lot of Indians that mother had sent out to hunt me. They said that Washakie was also out trying to find me. When I asked them what the Indians were going to do to me, they said that they would do nothing, that I had done what any of them would have done. I told them that I was afraid that it would start another camp fight, but they laughed and said it would not. This made me feel much better.

When I reached camp, mother asked me where I had been. I told her and she said I was a foolish boy for running away like that. "Well," I said, "I thought it might stop another camp fight if I went away."

It was not long before Washakie returned. He gave me a long talk, telling me not to run away any more but to come to him if I got into trouble again. He would see that I did not get hurt. I told him that I thought I had better go home, for I was always getting into trouble and making it hard for mother and him. He told me he would not let me go home for that, but advised me to be a little more careful, as I might have killed the boy. "A rope tied to a wild horse and around a boy's neck," he said, "is not much fun for the boy."

"Well I forgot about the rope's being tied to the horse," I said, "the boy made me so mad that I did not know what I was doing."

Washakie said that the boy's neck was badly skinned and that his father and mother were very angry about it, but that he would try to calm them. The other papooses who saw it thought that I did just right. The chief had a long talk with the boy's parents, and I heard no more about it, but I saw the boy wearing a greasy rag about his neck, and whenever I came near, he would look very savagely at me.

The mosquitoes made us move from this camp. We

Albert Schlechten, Bozeman, Mont.

A white-tailed deer.

went east nearly to the Teton Peaks, where we found game plentiful and the streams full of trout. The valley with its river running north and south through the middle of it was beautiful. There was no timber on the banks of the stream, but it was bordered with great patches of willows from one to two miles wide extending for about twenty miles along it. The white-tailed deer were plentiful among the willows. I killed five while we were there and mother tanned the skins and made a suit of clothes for me out of them. The clothes were nice and warm. The Indians also killed a number of moose among the willows.

Waskahie told me that his tribe had had a great fight with the Sioux Indians in this valley many years before when he was a small boy. He said that his people lost a great many of their best men. He took me all over the battle ground.

We stayed in this valley about thirty days and I began again breaking colts. When I brought up the first one, mother said, "Leave your rope here." I told her I could not manage the colt without it.

"Well, don't use it on any more papooses," she said, and I minded her.

The Indians killed a great many elk, deer, and moose while in this valley, and the squaws had all they could do tanning the skins and drying the meat. I asked Washakie if he was planning to winter in this valley.

"Oh, no," he replied. "The snow falls too deep here. After the buffalo get fat, and we kill all we want for our winter use, we will go a long way west out of the buffalo country, but where there are plenty of deer and antelope and fish. Some of the fish," he said, "are as long as you are."

Berries were getting ripe, so we papooses would go with

our mothers up in the hills and gather them to dry. It was great fun. One day, however, things got pretty exciting. We were in a canyon busy gathering the berries when all at once we heard a terrible screaming. Pretty soon there came a crowd of squaws and papooses. One was yelling, "A bear has killed my girl."

I jumped on my pinto pony, for I was riding him that day, and started up through the brush as fast as I could go. When I got a little way up the canyon, where the brush was not so thick, I could see a bear running up the hill. I went a little farther and found the girl stretched out on the ground as if she were dead. Then I shouted as loudly as I could for some of the Indians to come back, but they had all gone. I tried to lift her on to my horse but she was too heavy for me, so I laid her down again. Then she asked me for a drink. I took the cup she had been picking berries in and gave her some water. Then she said she felt better.

"Where is my mother?" she asked.

I told her that they had all run down the canyon like scared sheep. Then I helped her to her feet. She was crying all the time, and she said that her head and side and arm hurt her very much. I asked her if she could ride. She said she would try, so I helped her up on my horse and led it until we got out of the canyon. Then she told me to get on behind her as she thought she could guide the horse. We had about four miles to go, so I climbed upon the pony with her.

When we got in sight of camp we saw some Indians coming full tilt, and when they met us there was the greatest hubbub I ever heard. When we reached the camp the girl's mother came running up and threw her arms about the girl and acted as if she were crazy. She would have hugged me too if I had been willing. She

A black bear.

said that I was a brave boy.   Mother came up and said,
"Yagaki, I thought you had come down to camp ahead
of me or I never would have come without you."

"Oh, you were as scared as any of them," I said.

"I know I was scared," she said, "but I never
would have left you, if I had known you were still in
the canyon."

That night the girl's father and mother came to our
tepee to see what I wanted for saving their daughter's
life.   I told them that I wanted nothing.

"You are a good, brave boy," said her father.

I asked her mother why she ran away and left the girl.

"Well," she said, "I saw the bear knock my girl down
and jump on her and I thought she was dead, and I
thought the bear would kill me, then there would be two
of us dead."

The father said that the bears killed many people because they tried to help the one that was first caught.
He felt that it was better for the rest to run.   I did not

agree with him. I thought that everybody should help kill the bear even if they did run the risk of getting killed.

"Yes, you have already shown what you would do," said my mother. "You are a brave boy."

"It was a brave act for a boy," said Washakie; "but we must not brag too much about Yagaki or he will begin to think he is a great hero. It is about time we went to sleep."

The girl's mother told me that I might have her daughter for a wife when I got big enough; but I told her she could keep the girl, I did not want her.

The next day I wanted mother and the other Indians to go up the canyon after more service berries, but they wouldn't go a step. They had had bear scares enough for that time. The Indians left the bears alone unless they caught these animals in the open.

One morning we saw two bears crossing the valley. About fifty Indians on horses started after them. I ran and got my pinto pony. When I came back for my saddle, mother asked where I was going.

"To help kill those bears yonder."

"No, you are not," she said.

"Oh, let him go," said Washakie, and she consented. I jumped on the horse and started after the bears as hard as I could go. The Indians had headed them away from the timber and were popping arrows into them. My horse was not a bit scared so I ran up to one of the bears and shot three arrows into his side.

"Keep back, you little dunce," shouted the Indians, "that bear will tear you to pieces."

But the bear was too full of arrows to tear much. He looked like a porcupine with his quills on end. Very soon the two bears dropped dead; but their skins were so full

of holes that they were not worth much; the meat was not much good either.

That night the Indians had a big dance around the two hides. I joined in the fun and sang as loud as any of them. They thought I was pretty daring. One old Indian said, "The little fool doesn't know any better. If a bear once got hold of him he would not be so brave." But they gave me one of the hides and mother tanned it and sewed up most of the holes. It made me a very good robe to sleep in.

While we were in this valley another small band of Indians joined us. The girl that had hit me with the fishing pole was with them. When she saw that the other Indians liked me so much, she wanted to make up with me. She came around several times before she said anything to me, but finally one day she walked over to where I was helping mother stake down a moose hide to dry and said, "Yagaki, I am sorry that I hit you that day with the fish pole."

"I am not," I said.

"Why?" she asked.

"Because we had lots of fun that day."

"Why don't you be friends with her?" mother asked.

I said that I did not want to be her friend.

"You are a mean boy," said mother; "you should be friends."

"Not much," I said; but I did finally tell the girl that it was all right.

Then she wanted me to go over to their tepee and play, but I told her that I was afraid her mother would cut my head off.

"No," she said, "mother will not hurt you. She feels sorry for what we did to your folks, and so does my father."

Well, we passed the trouble over and became pretty good friends after that.

By this time we had gathered most of the berries that grew along the foothills; the squaws were afraid to go farther into the mountains after the bear excitement;

Creel

A squaw tanning buckskin.

so then they stopped berry picking and went to work in earnest tanning buckskin and drying meat for winter use. The Indians quit hunting for elk and deer; for they already had all of the skins that the women could get ready for the trading trip they had planned.

It was the custom of the tribe to make a journey almost every fall to Salt Lake City, and other White settlements, and swap their buckskin and buffalo robes for red blankets, beads, ammunition, and other things they needed. Mother and Hanabi worked all day and away into the night to get their skins ready in time, and I helped them all I could. I got an old horse and dragged down enough wood to last while we stayed there. I carried all the water for them, and no kid dared to call me a squaw either.

Finally the time came for us to begin killing buffaloes for our winter's supply of meat. We did not have to hunt them, however, for we could see them at any time in almost any direction. Many a time I went out with Washakie to watch the hunters kill the buffaloes. Washakie wanted only five and we soon got them; but it took mother and Hanabi a good many days to tan their hides and get the meat ready for winter.

"Three or four buckets of water came over me."

10   A LONG JOURNEY

NOTHING went wrong while we were getting ready for the long trip to market, and finally everything was in shape to pack up.   Our camp by this time was very large, for Indians had been coming in every few days until there were fully a thousand of them, and there must have been as many as five thousand horses.   When we took the trail, I could not see half of the long string of pack animals.

We had twenty pack horses for our own family, loaded with buffalo robes, elk and deer skins, and our camp outfit. Washakie had a fine big tepee of elk hides made so it would shed rain.   It could be divided in two parts. Sometimes if we were going to stop just one night, we would put up only half of it; but if we made a longer camp, we would set up the whole wigwam.

After we were well started, I noticed that the Indians broke up into small bands.   That night there were only twenty-five tepees left in our camp.   Washakie said that it was better to travel in small parties, for we could make better time and get better pasture for our horses.

In two or three days we reached the big river where I had come near choking the papoose to death with my rope. It was quite wide and the current was very swift where we forded it. When we got in the deepest place, mother's horse stumbled over a boulder and fell, and away went mother down the stream; for she could not withstand the swift current. I saw her going and started after her, but I could not catch her until she was carried into the deep, quieter waters. My horse was a good swimmer, and I was soon at her side. I pulled her to the bank and tried to help her out of the water, but the willows were so thick at this place we had a hard time getting on land. Washakie hurried to the rescue.

"You came nearly going to the Happy Hunting Grounds that time, mother," he said.

Washakie thought that we had better stop there so that mother could put on dry clothes and get over her scare, for he was afraid it would make her sick. We pitched camp for the night by a grove of cottonwoods near the river.

Just before dark an Indian came running in and told Washakie that the Crows had overtaken a small bunch of our Indians and had killed them and taken all their horses. Washakie ordered the War Chief to take every one of our warriors and follow the Crows clear into the Crow country if necessary to punish them. The War Chief told his men to get ready for a long trip, and the women and children to hide in the willows until they heard from them. I never saw greater excitement among the squaws and papooses than we had that night. They were bawling, and yelling, and rushing everywhere.

"Come on, Yagaki," called mother, "let us get into the brush."

"Not much," I said, "I am going with the warriors to kill Crows."

Mother grabbed me by one arm and Hanabi by the other, and mother began to cry and say to Washakie,

"Make him come; make him come."

Washakie laughed and said that I was just fooling, that I hadn't lost any Crows. He said that he was going to guard the camp.

"So am I," I said. With that mother let me go. I ran and caught my pinto pony, put my saddle and a few buffalo robes on him and went with mother and Hanabi down the river. When we reached the rest of the crowd, I could hear the papooses howling like a pack of young coyotes.

"What is the use of hiding and making such a racket?" I asked. "If the Crows have any ears they can hear this noise for five miles."

Mother said that it made no difference for the Crows did not dare to come into the brush after us.

"Are the Crows as big cowards as our Indians?" I asked.

She said that they were.

"Then there is no danger," I said; "we had better go to sleep."

It was not long before we heard Washakie call for us to come back.

"There," I said; "another scare is over with no Crows at all. I shall never hide again."

When we got to camp we learned that a few Crows had chased some of our Indians and had fired a few shots at them, but nobody had been killed, and not even a horse had been stolen. About fifty of our young warriors were following the Crows; but I knew that they would never overtake them.

The next day we packed up early and hit the trail pretty hard. For several days we headed south. We

E. S. Curtis

Indians traveling.

left the Piupa, or Snake River, and crossed over the mountains. Finally we came to a place called Tosaibi, which I learned later to be Soda Springs, in southeastern Idaho. We could not use the water of these springs, so we went on a short distance and camped on a good-sized river which the Indians called Titsapa; this was the Bear River.

They said that this stream ran into a big salt lake that reached nearly to my old home. That started me to thinking about my dear father and mother, my brothers and sisters I should like so much to see, and I could feel the tears running down my cheeks. Mother saw them and came and sat down by my side.

"Yagaki," she said, "I fear you do not like to live with us."

"Why do you say that?" I asked.

"What are you crying about?"

I told her that I was thinking of my white mother.

"Am I not as good to you as your own mother?" she asked.

I told her that she was. But I could not help wanting to see my white mother and my people just the same.

We followed down the Titsapa for one day's travel and there we stayed for three days. At this place part of our band was going to leave us and make the journey to Salt Lake City to sell our robes and buckskins and what furs we had. I wanted to go with the party, but mother would not let me. Hanabi and Washakie went. They took twelve pack horses very heavily loaded and also two young horses to sell if they got a chance. They left mother and me with the camp outfit and sixty-four head of horses to look after. Those that were not going to Salt Lake City intended to go off northwest and strike the head of another river, about four days' travel away, and stay there till the others returned.

When mother and I went to packing up for our return, we found that we did not have pack saddles enough for all of our camp outfit. Besides our tepee, bedding, clothing, and utensils, we had sixteen sacks of dried meat and two sacks of service berries. This was too much for our eight pack-saddles. Mother said that we could get along if we had two more saddles so I told her to use mine for one and I would ride bareback. She did not like to do this, but she finally consented, and another boy let us have his saddle, so we packed ten horses. This took a good deal of time each morning.

After three days of slow traveling we reached the head of a stream which they called Tobitapa; the whites now call it the Portneuf River. There were fifteen squaws, about thirty-five papooses, and three old men Indians in our camp.

Washakie thought it would take them fifteen days to go to Salt Lake City and get back to where we were. I asked mother whether she was not afraid that the Crows would come and kill all of us while they were gone.

"No," she said, "the Crows never come this far south."

Then I asked her why she did not want me to go to Salt Lake City with the others. She said that she could not take care of so many horses without me to help, and she was afraid, too, that the white men would take me away from her.

"Is that the reason Washakie does not like to take me with him when he goes among the whites?" I asked her.

She told me that Washakie said that if I ever got dissatisfied and wanted to go home, he would give me my horse and a good outfit, and see that I got home safe. "But," she said, "I hope that you will never want to go away, for I believe it would kill me if you should leave me." I told her not to worry because I thought that I should always stay with her. It always made her seem happier when I would tell her that. If she ever saw me look unhappy, she would turn away and cry. She did everything she could to make me happy, and I tried to be kind to her.

Mother was afraid that I would get sick from not having bread and milk to eat, for I told her that was what I always had for supper when I was home. She thought that eating meat all the time would not agree with me and would make me unhealthy. Often she would have fried fish and fried chickens or ducks for supper. When I first went to live with her, she made a small sack and tied it to my saddle. She would keep this sack full of the best dried fish when we were traveling, so that I could eat if I got hungry; for she said that I could not go all day without eating anything, as the Indians often did. Every morning she would empty my lunch sack and refill it with fresh food. She soon found out what I liked best, and she always had it for me; so you see I had plenty to eat, even if I was with Indians; and that is more than a great many white children had at that time.

I was very healthy while I was with the Indians. I think the reason was that I did not like their way of doctoring. When any of them got a cold, they would dig a hole two or three feet deep by the side of a cold spring. Into this hole they would put a few cobblestones. Then they would build a fire in the hole, get the stones right hot, and then scrape the fire all out. The sick person had to get into the hole with a cup of water, and after being covered with a buffalo robe, he would pour the water on the hot rocks and make a steam. This would make him sweat like sixty. When he had sweated long enough some one would jerk off the robe and he would jump into the cold water of the spring. As soon as he

Dr. T. M. Bridges

Indian sweat house covered; fire in foreground.

got out of the water, they would throw a buffalo robe around him, let him sweat awhile, then they would cool him off gradually by taking the robe off a little at a time while he quit sweating. He was then supposed to be well.

One chilly day I was out hunting chickens, and was quite a distance from camp when a heavy rainstorm came and soaked me through before I could get home. That night I coughed and coughed so that nobody in our tepee could sleep. The next day mother wanted to dig a hole for me. I told her that I did not want a hole dug for me until I was dead. She begged me to take a sweat.

"Not much," I said, "no more of your jumping into springs for me." I had not forgotten how they tried to cure my sore legs with a salt-springs bath.

She said that it would not hurt me. But I told her that I was played out and I would not do it.

"Well," she said, "you need not jump into the cold

water. The heat of the rocks and the steam from the ground will sweat you enough."

"You had better do it," said Washakie, "before you get sick in bed."

"All right," I said, "go to digging."

Very soon she had the hole dug and everything ready, then she said, "Come now, pull off your clothes and get in here."

"Pull off nothing," I said.

"You must," she said.

"Jerk them off," urged Washakie; "I will hold this buffalo robe over you so that you will not be seen."

So off came my clothes and into the hole I went. I got over the rocks just the way an old sitting hen does over her eggs. Mother gave me a cup of water and I poured it over the heated boulders. She stood there to keep the robe over the hole and kept asking me if I was sweating. I told her that I was getting wetter than a fish; but for

Dr. T. M. Bridges

Framework of an Indian sweat house.

some cause she kept me for quite a while, then she jerked off the robe and whack! three or four buckets of cold water came all over me. Oh, I jumped out of that hole in a hurry!

Washakie stood there with the robe, threw it over me, carried me into the tepee and put me to bed. Then he threw more robes over me, and how I did sweat! It was rough doctoring, but it cured my cold all right.

This was after Washakie and his party had got back from Salt Lake. They were gone twenty-two days instead of fifteen. Washakie had disposed of his robes and skins at a good price, and he had sold the two horses, so he came back pretty well outfitted for the winter. He had twenty-four blankets, a lot of calico, some red flannel for the tongues of moccasins, some underclothing for me, and about a peck of beads of all colors and sizes. The beads were to swap for tanned buckskin, and the blankets for buffalo robes. He brought me a butcher knife, a new bridle, two pounds of candy, and a lot of fishhooks. I felt "heap rich" and very happy.

11   THE SNOWY MOONS

Snow had already fallen on the mountain tops when Washakie got back, so he was in a hurry to get the camp moved to the winter range. Mother and Hanabi began at once to arrange the packs for traveling. We soon started for our winter quarters.

We went down the Tobitapa (Portneuf) to the Piupa (Snake River), then up the Piupa, and then west over the divide on to the headwaters of Angitapa (Rock Creek). At this place we stayed six days and killed sixteen buffaloes, two for each family. That was to be the last killing of buffaloes until the next year. Washakie bought four of the buffalo hides from other Indians, which made six in all. He said that he wanted something for the women to do through the winter.

When we started from here we went west over a big mountain upon which we had to camp in about three feet of snow. We had to tie up all our horses to keep them from running away, for we had nothing for them to eat. Early the next morning we were off and that night we got out of the snow, but it was still very cold. The next day we came to a beautiful stream. It was not very large, but it was fairly alive with mountain trout. We went down the stream two days' travel and there we stayed for about a month, I think. Washakie had intended to winter here, but he changed his mind and followed the stream farther down until he came to another river. I do not remember what the Indians called this river, but they told me that fish as long as I was tall came up the river in the springtime. We had a very good camping ground that winter. It was sheltered from the wind, but we had a great deal more snow than had fallen the winter before.

About six hundred yards above our camp was a large grove of dry quaking aspens, mostly small poles. I told mother that if she would help me pile a lot of them, I would haul them down with the horses. She did not believe that I could do it, but she helped me gather the poles just the same.

Washakie had brought from Salt Lake City the inch auger I asked him to get for me, so I went to work to make a sled like the one I had seen my father make. I got two crooked sticks for runners, pinned on some cross pieces, and soon had the thing ready. It did not look much like a sled, but it answered the purpose pretty well.

I got up two lazy old horses of mother's, put on their pack saddles and tied ropes from the sleds to the pack saddles, then I mounted one of the horses and away we went for the grove. After putting on quite a few poles and tying them on with a rope, I took the load to camp without any bother at all. All of the Indians were out watching me bring in my first load of wood.

"What cannot a white man do?" said the old War Chief.

In a few days I had all of the wood we needed down to the camp. Hanabi said that I was as good as two squaws. After getting our wood up, I lent the sled to some of the Indians. They thought they could haul wood as well as I could, so they hitched up their horses and started out. But they went on higher up the hill where it was steeper than where I got my wood. Then they put on a big load and started down. The sled ran into the horses' heels, scared them, and they started to run. The horse that the Indian was riding broke loose from the sled, and the other horse ran away with the sled fastened to him, scattering the poles all over the side of the hill, and bolting down through the camp. The sled jammed against the tepees and jerked three or four of them down. Then the frightened horse struck out through some cottonwoods, slammed the sled against the trees, and broke it all to pieces.

Shoshone tepee with sagebrush windbreak.

This discouraged the Indians. They said that the squaws could pack wood if they wanted any, that it was their work anyhow. That ended the wood hauling.

I got the Indian boys to help me fix up the sled again. We pulled it up on a hill with a horse and turned it towards camp. I wanted some of the boys to get on with me and slide down, but they were afraid. They said they wanted to see me do it first, so away I went. Then they came down with the horse and we pulled the sled up again. By hard begging, I got two of them on the sled. As soon as we started, one jumped off, but the other stayed with me. When we reached the bottom, he said it was the finest ride he ever had. The next time several of the boys were ready to try it, and five of us got on. Away we went to the bottom. Oh, what fun we had! It was not long till they all wanted to get on, and the heavier we loaded it, the faster it would go. When the track got slick, the sled would carry us nearly to camp.

We kept this up for days. When the track was well made, we would pull the sled up without a horse. All of the big boys and girls joined in the coasting, and sometimes the older Indians would ride too. The sled was kept going all the time, until we wore the runners out. After that for fun we turned to fishing and hunting chickens and rabbits. Sometimes we would go for antelope, but when we went for them, some of the older Indians would go with us to keep us from killing too many. The Indians were always careful to preserve the game.

Everything went off peacefully this winter. There was no quarreling nor fighting. One young papoose and an old squaw died. We lost no horses. We were a long way from the Crows, so we had no Crow scares. I had a very good time, and mother seemed to enjoy the winter as well as I did.

Along towards spring seven or eight of us little boys were in the cottonwoods shooting birds when one boy's arrow hit the side of a tree, glanced, and struck me in the leg. The boy was badly scared, for he thought I was going to kick him to pieces, but I told him to stop crying, that I knew it was an accident. He quit crying, and the other boys thought that I was getting to be a pretty good fellow after all, for before this they believed that if any one hurt me there would be a kicking scrape right away.

Spring came at last. We moved down the river about fifteen miles where we could get better grass for our horses. Here were plenty of white-tailed deer and antelope, some elk, and a few mountain sheep. Ducks and geese also were plentiful.

We stayed here until about the middle of May. The big fish they had told me about began to come up the river. And they were really big ones; two of them made all the load I could carry. They must have weighed thirty or thirty-five pounds each. Mother and Hanabi dried about two hundred pounds of these fish. I afterwards learned that they were salmon. The first that came up were fat and very good, but they kept coming thicker and thicker until they were so thin that they were not fit to eat.

After a while we moved camp again, going down the river a little farther and then up a deep and rocky canyon where there had been many snowslides during the winter. We crossed over snow that had come down in these slides that was forty or fifty feet deep and was as hard as ice. There was not very much timber in the canyon, and the cliffs were very high. Years afterwards very rich gold mines were found in this place, a mining camp was started, and great quartz mills were built.[1]

[1] Virginia City, Montana.

Lee Moorhouse

" The burden bearer "— Squaw carrying wood.

As we left the canyon, we climbed a very steep mountain for about two miles, and then went down through
thick timber until we came out on to a beautiful prairie
covered with the finest grass I had ever seen. Off to
the left was a deep canyon where one fork of the Big
Hole River headed, and here we camped for a long time.
The Indians killed a great many black-tailed deer and
antelope and dried the meat. I think Washakie and I
killed seventeen while we stayed here.

Our next move was down to the forks of the river, where
we stayed three or four weeks to give the women time to tan
the deerskins. It was fine fishing in the Big Hole River.

While we were staying here, one of the War Chief's boys was accidentally shot and killed. Oh, what crying we had to do! Every one in camp who could raise a yelp had to cry for about five days. I had to mingle my gentle voice with the rest of the mourners. They killed three horses and buried them and his bow and arrows with him. The horses were for him to ride to the Happy Hunting Grounds. When they got ready to bury him, every one in camp had to go up to him and put a hand on his head and say he was sorry to have him leave us. When it came my turn, I went into our tepee and would not come out. Mother came after me. I told her I would not go, that I was not sorry to see him go, for he was no good anyhow.

"Don't say that so they will hear it," she said. Then she went back and made excuses for me.

They took him up to a high cliff and put him in a crevice with his bedding, a frying pan, an ax, his bow and arrows, and some dried buffalo meat. After this they covered him with rocks. When they got back to camp, they let out the most pitiful howls I ever heard. I joined them too, just as loud as I could scream, as if I was the most broken-hearted one in the camp, but it seemed so foolish to keep up this howling, as they did for five days. I got so hoarse I could hardly talk.

But I did feel sorry for his poor mother. She was really grief-stricken. She cut off her hair close to her head. I asked mother why she did that. She said that all mothers did it when their oldest boy died. After our mourning was over, she would still weep bitterly and sometimes scream out her sorrow.

We next moved down the Big Hole River to where the town of Melrose is now situated. We stayed here for about two weeks, then went on till we came to where the

Caspar W. Hodgson

Coming in from an antelope hunt on Camas Prairie, Idaho, years ago before these pronghorns were fully protected.

Big Hole empties into the Beaver Head River and forms the Jefferson River.

Here we did nothing but fish. The buffalo were not fat enough to kill, and besides, we had all of the dried elk and deer meat we wanted. It was a beautiful place to camp, and we had the finest of grass for our horses.

I broke a few more colts, two for mother and four for Washakie. Our horses by this time were getting fat and looking fine, but my little pinto was the prettiest one of all. Hardly a day passed but some Indian would try to trade me out of him. One Indian offered me two good horses if I would swap, but I thought too much of the pony to part with him even for a whole band of horses. He was just as pretty as a horse could be.

Our next journey took us a long way northeast. Washakie said that we were going where the buffaloes were too many to count. After about a week of travel, we reached the north fork of the Madison River, about on a line with the Yellowstone Park; and oh, the kwaditsi (antelope) and padahia (elk) and kotea (buffalo) there were! Every way we looked we could see herds of them.

While we were at this camp another boy was killed by a horse. He was dragged almost to pieces through the rocks and brush.

When I heard of it, I told mother to get her voice ready for another big howling.

"Aren't you ashamed to talk that way?" asked Hanabi.

"I am afraid you are a hard-hearted boy," said mother.

After the poor fellow was buried, we went up the Madison River about ninety miles and camped there for a month. The buffalo were now in better condition, so we killed a good many, drying their meat and making their hides into robes. Then we went on south and came to the beautiful lake where we had had such a good time the summer before.   It is now called Henry's Lake, and is the head of the north fork of the Snake River.   We did nothing here but fish, for we had enough dried meat to last till we reached the usual hunting grounds.

12   THE FIERCE BATTLE

We were now traveling towards the Crow country. I think our Indians were a little afraid that the Crows were going to try to stop them ; but Washakie said that he was going through if it cost him half of his tribe, for he was not going to be bluffed off his best hunting ground any longer.

I thought something was up, because small bands of Indians kept joining us, until we had gathered about seven hundred warriors. We sent all of our surplus horses down the Snake River with Indians to guard them until we came back. Washakie and mother kept fifteen head for pack horses, and I kept two horses to ride. After the extra horses and packs had gone, we started for the disputed hunting grounds.

The men all went out ahead, followed by the pack horses, with the women and children and old men in the rear. Mother warned me to keep close to her, for Washakie said that the Crows might tackle us that day. I said that kind of talk was too thin. But we had not been traveling very long before one of our scouts came tearing back and said that he had seen where a very large band of Crows had passed, and had sighted smoke in the timber ahead.

The men all stopped and bunched together. I heard Washakie tell them to go ahead, to keep a good lookout, and if the Crows pounced on them, to fight as long as there was a man left. I thought that they must be getting brave.

We started again with the men in the lead as before, but riding very slowly. Six or eight Indians kept riding back and forth along our line to keep the squaws and pack horses from getting scattered.

Pretty soon we stopped again and the War Chief ordered us to camp there for the night. "We know now," he said, "that we must fight or go back, and we have gone back so much that the Crows begin to think we are afraid of them. I feel that we ought to give them a lesson this time that they will not forget soon."

"That is the way I look at it," said Washakie. "Now is the time to show them that we will fight for our rights."

This seemed to be the way most of the warriors felt, for I heard them talking about it in their council that night.

We camped right there, all in a bunch, with hardly room to make down our beds. A strong guard was sent to look after the horses, but the night passed off without any trouble. When morning came, ten men were sent to see if they could find any signs of the Crows. They were gone about an hour, when back they came and reported that about a thousand Crows were camped over the ridge just ahead of us.

"We will go on to our hunting grounds," said the War Chief, "if there are ten thousand of them."

The Indians painted up in grand style. They drew black streaks all over their faces to make themselves look fiercer, and then we got ready and started forward. We had not gone far when the squaws were ordered to stop. The warriors went on and passed over a small ridge out of our sight.

Pretty soon we heard shooting, then an Indian came and told us to go back until we came to good water and stay there until we heard from the chief. "They are fighting now," he said.

We had hardly reached the stream of water before we saw Indians come up on the hill and then disappear, then come in sight again. They seemed to be fighting fiercely, and they were yelling to beat Old Billy. They had not been fighting over an hour before half or two thirds of them were on top of the hill and slowly coming down the side towards us.

The squaws began to cry and say that the Crows were getting the better of our Indians and were driving them

Dr. T. M. Bridges

A Shoshone brave (Fort Hall, Idaho).

back. They kept coming closer and closer to us. When
I looked around I saw that the squaws were getting their
butcher knives; they were ready to fight if they had to.
Then I noticed that our men were not coming towards
us any longer. I could see Washakie on his big buckskin
horse dashing around among the Indians and telling them
what to do, and very soon the driving turned the other
way; they began to disappear over the ridge again, and
I could tell that our Indians were beating the Crows.

We could tell the Crow Indians from ours, for they
had something white over one shoulder and under one
arm, and they wore white feathers in their hair. There
were about fifteen hundred Indians engaged in the fight
on both sides, as the battle ground covered quite a piece
of country. We could see a good many horses running
around without riders.

I believe that the squaws would have taken part in
the battle if it had not been for the guard of about fifty
old Indians that kept riding around us all the time to
keep the squaws and papooses and horses close together.

When our men had driven the Crows back to the ridge,
they seemed to stick there; but they were still fighting
and yelling and circling around. It looked as if they
could not force the enemy back any farther. I got so
excited that I jumped on my horse and said to another
Indian boy, "Come on, let's go up and see what they are
doing and try to help them."

Mother grabbed my bridle and said, "You crazy little
dunce; haven't you one bit of sense?"

"I might kill a whole flock of Crows," I said, "for
all you know." But she would not let me go, and I
guess it was a good thing I did not.

After about six hours of fighting, one Indian, badly
wounded, came in and told us to go back to the lake, but

not to unpack until we got word from the War Chief. We went back and when we got to the top of the divide we could still see the Indians fighting, although they were about two miles away, and we could see loose horses all over the prairie. The sun was nearly an hour high when we reached the lake.

About dark half of our Indians came to us and the War Chief told us to unpack and put up the tepees, for very likely we should stay there for a while. He told us that about sundown the Crows broke and ran and that Washakie with the other half of our Indians was following them to try to head them off and keep them from getting away. Washakie thought that he and his warriors could stop them until morning, and then all of his band could attack them again. The War Chief sent twenty Indians with one hundred fresh horses to overtake the Indians that were following the Crows, for their horses had been on the go all day and were about worn out. He said that he had seen twenty-five of our Indians that were dead. How many more had been killed he did not know. Mother told them that they might take two of her horses and I let them have my roan pony to help them in their chase after the fleeing Crows.

By this time three or four hundred squaws and papooses were wailing and moaning till they could be heard for two miles. I asked mother when our turn would come.

"Do hush and go to sleep," said Hanabi; but there was not much sleep that night.

When day came, I saw such a sight as I had never seen before. About one hundred Indians had been brought in during the night, all very badly wounded. Mother and I went around to see them. One poor fellow had his nose shot off and one eye shot out. He said he didn't

feel very well. Many of them were so badly hurt **that** I knew they could not live until sundown, and I thought about half of them would die that day. A few old **Indians** were sent over to the battle field to keep the eagles and wolves from eating the Indians that had been killed. The War Chief had been shot in the arm and in the leg, but was not very badly hurt. He had gone before I got up that morning and had taken with him all of the **war-** riors that were able to go.

That night a little after dark all of our Indians re- turned. Washakie said that the Crows had gone into the thick timber from which he could not get them out, but that there were not many of them left anyhow. Our men brought in a very large band of Crows' horses and saddles and when they were unpacked I never before saw such a pile of buffalo robes, blankets, bows **and** arrows, and guns. The next morning we all started out for the battle ground to bury our dead and oh, what a sight! There were Indians scattered everywhere all over the battle field. The squaws and papooses wailed pitifully when they saw their dead Indians lying around. Wives were hunting for their husbands; mothers were looking for their sons.

I went about picking up arrows. I had gathered quite a few when mother saw me with them.

"Throw them down quick," she said, "the old Indians will come around and gather them. Don't touch anything."

"What do they want with them?" I asked.

"They will keep them for another fight," was her answer.

The squaws scalped every Crow they could find.

"Why don't you scalp our Indians and send their scalps to the Crows?" I asked her.

"Go away," she said, "you don't know what you are talking about."

Our Indians carried our dead to a deep washout in the side of the hill, put them in and covered them with dirt and rocks. The dead Crows were left to the wolves and the buzzards.

That night when I got back to camp I was very tired and hungry, and I had seen so many Indians scalped that I felt sick and wished from the bottom of my heart that I was home with my kindred.

About two hundred and fifty horses were captured from the Crows. Thirty-one Indians on our side had been killed and about one hundred wounded. Eighteen of these afterwards died from their wounds, making forty-nine in all we lost in that terrible fight. The Crows had suffered far worse than we did. The men sent out by Washakie to count the killed came back and reported that they had found one hundred and three dead Crows. Washakie thought this number would be increased greatly by those that died from their wounds.

I began to change my mind about our Indians being cowards after seeing that fight. I have seen other fights between the whites and the Indians, but I never have seen greater bravery displayed than was shown by our Indians in this fierce battle with the Crows.

We had to stay in this place about three weeks to give our wounded warriors a chance to get well. When we could move them, it was too late to go the rounds that Washakie had planned, so we began to get ready for winter. Our camp was moved over on the Angatipa (Rock Creek), and the hunters began to kill buffaloes while the squaws dried the meat. There were a good many widows and orphans now to take care of. The worst of it was the man who was best at cutting the hamstrings had been killed in battle, so we could not get on so fast with our hunting. However, we soon got all of the buffaloes that we wanted and the squaws began to make the hides into robes.

Poor old mother and Hanabi worked very hard to get ours ready for the journey to Salt Lake. Washakie had a good many robes. Besides those he had got from hunting, he had bought a lot from other Indians, and he had his chief's share of those captured from the Crows. We had six packs of dried meat and our camp outfit made three more. Altogether it made so heavy a load that we could not travel very fast.

When we got over the divide Washakie said that mother and I had better stay there with some of the others to take care of the extra horses. I did not like to do this, for I wanted to go to Salt Lake this time; but I would do anything that Washakie advised. He told us that we could come on slowly after them.

When they started for Salt Lake, they took with them about thirty head of the Crows' horses to swap for anything they could get for them. After they were gone, there were one hundred of us left behind, mostly squaws and papooses and old and wounded Indians to take care of, besides six hundred head of horses.

Bur. Am. Ethnology, Smithsonian Institution
Chief Washakie (center) and two of his Shoshone braves (Wyoming).

13   LIVELY TIMES

AFTER the trading party had been gone two days, the rest of our band moved down the creek to where it sank in the sand hills.   Here three of the wounded Indians got so bad that we had to stop for some time; but we had the finest of grass for our horses, and the sage hens were as thick as could be.

One day I was out shooting chickens.   I had killed four with arrows and was coming home, when, as I was passing a tepee, a dog jumped out and got me by the leg.   He tore off quite a piece of my flesh and I shot him through with an arrow, leaving the feathers on one side of him and the spike sticking out of the other.   As I was trying to catch the dog to get my arrow back, the old squaw that owned him ran up with a rope.   She threw it over my head and jerked me along to her tepee. And there she held me while her girl tied my feet and hands.   Then the angry old squaw grabbed a butcher knife and was going to cut my head off.

A sick Indian, who happened to be lying near by,

jumped up and held the squaw while a little boy ran and told mother. Mother came in double quick time. She grabbed the knife from the squaw, cut the strap that she had tied me with, took me by the arm, and made me hike for my tepee. When she saw how the dog had bitten me, oh, she was mad. She went back to the squaw, with me following her, and said: "If you don't kill that dog before sundown, I will kill you. Look here, see this poor boy with his leg nearly bitten off."

The old Indians that had gathered around stopped the fracas, or I guess there would have been another camp fight.

Mother went for the medicine man. When he came he said that it was a very bad bite, and that we must be very careful or blood poison would set in. He said that the dog would have to be killed. I told him that I thought the dog would die if they let him alone.

"But he must be killed before he dies," said the medicine man.

This made me laugh.

The cut in my leg was "V" shaped, and the piece of flesh hung only by the skin.

"Ouch!" I cried, when he tried to put it back in place.

"What did you say?" he asked.

"Ouch!"

"What is that?"

"I don't know."

"Oh," he said, going on with his work of patching up my leg. He put the piece back where it belonged and tied it there with a piece of something; then he got some weeds, mashed them up and made a poultice and put it on the wound.

After this he went to have the dog killed. I told him to hurry up or the dog would be dead before he got there.

When the medicine man told any one to do anything, he had to do it. He sent a big boy to kill the dog, but when the boy got to the tepee, the old squaw and her girl pitched on to him and beat the poor fellow nearly to death. Then the medicine man sent two big Indians to see what they could do. When they reached the place, I could hear very loud talking, so I got up and went to the door to see the fun. One Indian had hold of the old squaw; the other had the girl and they were shaking them to beat time. I was glad of it. They deserved a good shaking.

Well, they killed the dog before he died, anyway.

When the camp had quieted down again, the medicine man came and changed the poultice on my leg. It had swollen very badly by this time. He told mother to boil sage leaves and with the tea to bathe my leg very often. I could hear mother crying while she was out gathering the sage, and when she came in I asked her what she was crying about. She said she was afraid that I should be lame all my life from the hurt. I told her that I should be well in a week, that a little thing like that would not make me lame very long; but my leg pained me so that I did not get much sleep that night.

The next morning the squaw and her girl and their tepee were gone, but the sick Indian was left lying there alone in his bed. I told mother to let him come into our tepee and stay until his squaw got back. She had gone with Washakie to sell her robes and skins, and had left her sister-in-law to take care of her wounded husband until she returned. Mother objected to taking care of him, but when I told her he had saved my life by keeping that old squaw from cutting my head off, she consented and asked him to come over to our tepee.

The poor old fellow was very sick and so weak he could

hardly walk. He had been shot three times with arrows — in the arm, in the leg, and in his side. The wound in his side was so bad that the medicine man had to take out part of his two ribs. It kept the medicine man busy tending to me and all of the wounded Indians.

Mother bathed my sore leg three times a day with sage tea; the swelling all went away, and I was getting along fine. In about a week I had mother get me some sticks and I made some crutches; then I could get around out of doors. When the other lame Indians saw how well I could move about, they had me make them crutches also, so that they could move about.

After staying here nearly two weeks, we had to move, for the wood was getting scarce close to camp. I hobbled around and helped mother pack up; then we went over through the sand hills and came to a good-sized stream which they called Tonobipa. The stream ran south through the sand hills and lava beds, and farther down it sank out of sight into the ground.

The sick Indians had a hard time while we were on the move, but I stood the trip very well. After staying in our new camp for four days, we packed up again and started for the place where we were to meet Washakie. That was five days' travel away. We could not travel very fast on account of the sick Indians and we could not get a very early start because of having so many horses to pack, so it seemed a very long journey.

One day we had to make a twenty-five-mile ride to reach water. That day was too hard on our sick. We were obliged to leave two of them in the sand hills, while we pushed on to the Piupa. One old Indian carried water back to them. It was way after dark when we got to the river. Oh, how tired I was, and how my leg did hurt before that day's travel was over. I was glad to get a good drink of water and to lie down to rest. My leg hurt so much that mother would not let me do a thing. She unpacked all the horses and put up the tepee alone.

The medicine man came to take care of my leg. When he unwrapped it to put on another poultice, he found that it had turned black. He said that it had begun to mortify and would have to be cut off. Then mother began to cry so hard that the whole camp heard her, and several Indians came up to see what was the matter. She told them that her poor boy must lose his leg.

"Not by a blame sight!" I said. Then I told the old medicine man to pike away to his tepee and not to come back any more. Mother cried harder and begged him not to go. She said that I was out of my head and did not know what I was saying.

"Yes, he does," said the old rascal, "and I do not care if the little white devil does die."

"I know you don't," I replied; "if you did, you would not want to cut my leg off. I know very well what I am saying," I told him; "now you get, and mighty quick, too, or when Washakie comes I'll have him cut both your legs off."

Away he went as mad as fire. When he had gone mother said, "Now you have run the medicine man off, you will die."

"Not half so quick as I would if he kept putting his poisoned poultices on my leg," I said. "I should have been well long ago if he had left me alone. He has been trying to kill me ever since he began to doctor me. I am not going to let him do anything for me any more."

Mother gathered more sage and bathed my leg. The poor old woman worked with me nearly all night, and the next morning my leg was better, but I could not move it

without a great deal of pain. Mother said that we should
not leave that place until I got well even if it took all
winter. The next morning, when mother got up she
said she dreamed that Washakie came and killed a sage
hen and put the entrails on my leg and it cured it right
away. I told her to keep right on with sage tea, and I
thought it would be all right soon.

After we had been here a few days, some of the Indians
wanted to go on to the place where we were to meet
Washakie; but mother said she would not move until
I got better, so five tepees stayed with us and the rest
went on. Washakie and his party were at the rendezvous
waiting for them. When they told him how I was, he
started out, and in two days he reached our camp.

The chief was very angry when he saw my leg and was

told how I had been treated. It was bad enough, he said, to be bitten by a dog without having the squaw threaten to kill me. He said that she would have to leave the tribe. When I told him how the old medicine man had acted, he was angrier still.

The chief had left his things in bad shape; he wanted to go back as soon as I could be moved. I told him I thought I could travel, so the next morning we packed up for the start; but as I went to get on my horse it hurt my leg so much that I began to cry.

"Hold on," said Washakie, "I will fix things so you can ride better." Then he and some more Indians tied some tepee poles on each side of two horses and wove some rope between the poles, making a kind of litter. Several buffalo robes were thrown on the rope net and this made a fine bed. Mother led the front horse and away we went in first-class style. After we got going, Washakie came up and asked me whether they were traveling too fast.

"No," I said, "you can run if you want to."

He laughed and said that I was all right.

That day mother got some boys to shoot some sage hens for her. They killed three and when we camped she put the entrails on my sore leg. I slept well that night. It was the first good sleep I had had for more than a week. As we traveled along, mother took good care of my leg in this way and by the time we got to the main camp I could walk again on my crutches.

The next morning after we arrived here, Washakie told the War Chief to send down the river for the best medicine man in the tribe. I told Washakie that I would not let any more of his medicine men fool with my leg. He said that he only wanted him to see it. That day the good medicine man came, and when he saw my leg, he shook his head and said that it was a wonder I was alive, for the old medicine man had been putting poison weeds on it, and if he had kept it up two days longer I would have been dead.

Washakie sent for the old medicine man. When he came the chief asked him, "What have you been doing with this boy?"

He said that he had been doing all he could for me.

"I don't want any more of your lies," said Washakie. "If this boy had died, I would have had you tied to the tail of a wild horse and let him kick and drag you to death. Now, go, and don't let me see you any more, for you are hated by every Indian, squaw, and papoose in this camp."

We stayed in this place till my leg got nearly well, then we moved on down the river to stop for the winter. Here the fishing was good, and the white-tailed deer, ducks, and rabbits were very plentiful.

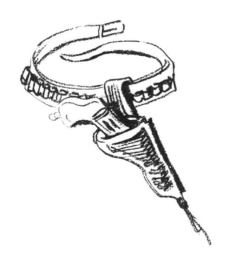

14   OLD MOROGONAI

DURING the time that I was disabled and had to stay in the tepee, my old friend, Morogonai, would come and talk to me for hours.   He told me all about the first white men he ever saw.   It was Lewis and Clark.   When they made their trip across the continent, this old Indian had sold them some horses, and had traveled with them for about ten days, catching fish and trading them to the whites for shirts and other articles.

Old Morogonai was respected by all the tribe.   He had once been a chief among the Shoshones, but now that he was too old to lead the Indians, he became an arrow-maker for them.

I used to like to watch him make arrows.   It takes skill to make a good one.   Our Indians generally used the limbs of service-berry bushes for this purpose.   They would cut a great many of these and leave them for a year to dry thoroughly.   Old Morogonai would take a bundle of these seasoned limbs and draw each one through a hole in an antelope horn to make it perfectly straight.

Then he would crease each shaft, and after this he would feather them and put on the steel spikes. In earlier times they used flint heads, which they had chipped into shape. If the arrow was for long-distance shooting, the feathers were made heavier than the spike; if for short distances, the spike was made heavier so that it would bring the arrow down more quickly.

The bows were sometimes made of mountain sheep horns, which were thrown into some hot spring and left there until they were pliable. Then they were shaped, and a strip of sinew was stuck on the back with some kind of balsam gum that was about as good as glue. This made a powerful bow. Not many Indians had this kind; most of our Indians used bows made from white cedar strung with sinew along the back.

For other weapons, the Indians had spears made of small pine-tree shafts about twelve feet long and a steel spike about four inches in length. When they were not using their spears, they would take the spike off the shaft, sharpen it, and keep it in a little buckskin scabbard. They traded with the whites for knives and tomahawks and guns.

Old Morogonai told me many things about his experiences with the white man. He was not unfriendly towards them, but he felt that they had often mistreated the Indians, and caused a good deal of unnecessary suffering and trouble for both the red men and the whites.

"At one time," he said, "an emigrant train, on its way to Oregon, camped at Humboldt Springs. Some of Pocatello's Indians went to the camp to swap buckskins for flour. The white men took three of their squaws and drove the rest of the Indians away. That made the Indians mad. They gathered a large band of Indians, followed the train, and killed every one of the white men in it. Then they took all their stock and clothing and food and weapons, and afterwards set fire to the wagons."

"At another time," he said, "some mail carriers drove a band of fine big horses up to my camp of Indians and asked me to take care of the animals for them for two moons, then they would come and give us fifteen red blankets. They had stolen the horses from an emigrant train. We did not know this, however, so we agreed to take care of the animals for them.

"In a few days the emigrants found the tracks of their horses around our camp and thinking we had stolen them, they began to shoot before they gave my Indians a chance to explain. After shooting seven of my braves, they rode off, driving with them not only their own horses but some of ours.

"I was away at the time with most of my men. When I returned, I found my oldest boy and five other Indians dead and another dying. I gathered what was left of my band and that night we set out in hot pursuit of the whites; but it was eight days before I got a chance to get even. There were a good many men in the camp and they kept a strong guard at night. On the eighth night it grew very stormy, we skipped in through the darkness, stampeded their horses, and got away with twenty-two of them. The whites followed us, and they would have overtaken us, if we had not run into a large camp of Pocatello's Indians. We did not stop, but kept right on going.

"When the emigrants came up to Pocatello's band, they pitched into these Indians without waiting for explanations. A big fight followed and men were killed on both sides, but the Indians finally got the worst of it. The best of it was that we got away with the horses.

"After we got back to the main tribe, Washakie happened to hear about the trouble and he sent for me. I

Dr. T. M. Bridges

"Old Ocean" (at right), one of the Lewis and Clark Shoshone guides. This picture was taken about 1885, when the noted Indian guide was more than one hundred years old.

told him the full story. He said that he did not blame me; but it was a bad scrape and he did not want any trouble with the whites.

"He advised me to keep away from the road where the white men travel, and have nothing to do with them; 'for,' said he, 'they have crooked tongues; no one can believe what they have to say.'"

"We did not know," said the old arrow-maker, "what whooping cough, measles, and smallpox were until the whites brought these diseases among us. A train of emigrants once camped near us ; some of their white papooses had the whooping cough ; our papooses caught it from them. Our medicine man tried to cure it as he would a bad cold, and more than half of our papooses died from the disease and the treatment. Hundreds of our people have been killed with the smallpox brought to us by the white man. ·

"The white men keep crowding the Indians that are east of here out west, and they keep crowding us farther west. Very soon they will have us away out in Nevada where there is nothing but lizards and snakes and horned toads to live on. If they crowd us farther than that, we shall have to jump off into the Great Water."

When Old Morogonai was telling me these and other tales about the cruel wrongs the Indians have suffered from the whites, I was not prepared to sympathize with him as I can now. But I have seen so much since on both sides that I am sure he told me the truth. Most of the

Bur. Am. Ethnology, Smithsonian Institution

Family of Bannock Indians of Pocatello's tribe, about 1860.

Shoshone and Bannock Indian relics collected by Dr. T. M. Bridges.

trouble between the whites and the Indians has been caused by the white men, who had not white hearts; they did not treat the Indian fairly.

I know that the Indians were a treacherous and revengeful people. They always demanded a life to pay for a life, and they would often do bloodthirsty things. But the whites were mostly to blame. If they had been fair with the Indians, and treated them kindly, instead of taking mean advantages of them, the Indians would have been kind and friendly. I cannot blame the Indians as much as some do. They were good friends to me, and most of them have peaceful hearts.

"The War Chief asked me some more questions."

15   THE BIG COUNCIL

OUR winter camp was a very beautiful place with plenty of game and an abundance of good dry wood. We had nearly everything that was needed to make us happy. My leg and all of the sick Indians got well, and we were getting along finely when one day some of Pocatello's Indians came to our camp.

That night Washakie called a council of the tribe to meet in the War Chief's tepee. I thought this strange, for he had always held his councils in our tepee. The next morning they held another council, so I thought I would go over and see what it was all about. But when I got to the door of the council tepee, I met an Indian who told me to run back, that they did not want me in there. This puzzled me, for I had never before been sent away from the councils.

When I got back to our tepee, mother and Hanabi were both crying. I knew then that something serious was up, but they would not tell me a word about it.

112

I thought that Pocatello's Indians wanted Washakie to help them in some bloody affair with the whites.

Things went on in this way for four days. The Indians kept on holding councils, but I could not learn what was the cause. I saw other squaws come to our tepee, but when I came near them, they would stop talking. This made me think that the trouble had something to do with me, and I worried a good deal about it.

On the fifth morning Washakie sent for me. I went and found about fifteen Indians at the council. The War Chief first asked me how old I was.

"About fourteen years," I answered.

"How old were you when you left home?" he went on.

"Nearly twelve."

"Were you stolen away or did you come to us of your own accord?" was his next question.

I told him that I ran away; nobody forced me to come; but two Indians coaxed me and gave me my pinto pony.

He then told me that I might go. When I got back to our tepee mother and Hanabi wanted to know what had happened and I told them.

That night the council was continued in Washakie's tepee. The War Chief asked me some more questions. He wanted to know how the Indians treated me, and why I ran away from home.

I told him that I had been treated just as well by the Indians as I had ever been treated by the whites, and that I ran away because I was tired of herding sheep alone. Besides, I wanted the pinto pony and the only way I could get him was to go with the Indians, so I went.

"Have the Indians kept their promises with you?" the War Chief asked.

"They have done everything they said they would do," I told him; "I haven't any fault to find with them."

Bur. Am. Ethnology, Smithsonian Institution

Shoshone War Chief's tepee, from a photograph taken in 1861. The tepee is made of buffalo skins, and is possibly the identical one in which the big council was held.

Washakie then said that he had told the Indians they might offer me the pony if I would come; but they were not to force me away from home. "So when he came," the chief continued, "we gave the squaw who owned the pinto four colts for him. I gave her a yearling, mother gave two others, and Morogonai gave one. We never told the boy that he could have the pony; but we all understood that it belonged to him. Afterwards I gave him another horse for breaking some colts for me."

The War Chief asked me whether I would rather live with the white people or the Indians. I told him I would sooner live with the Indians. With that the council broke up and the Indians went to their various tepees.

"What does all this mean?" I asked Washakie.

"You will know in the morning," he replied.

"If they intend to take my pony away," I said, "I will skip out in the night."

"They are not going to do that," said my mother; "whenever you go, that horse goes with you."

We all went to bed that night wondering what would happen next day. It was a long night for me, for I did not sleep much.

Morning came at last, and after breakfast the War Chief with several other Indians came to our tepee. With them were the Pocatello Indians. When they were all inside the tepee, Washakie told me that these Indians had been down to the place where my people lived; that my father said I had been stolen by the Indians; that he was raising a big army to come and get me; and that he was going to kill every Indian he could find. Washakie asked me what I thought about it. I told him that it was not so.

"In the first place," I said, "my people do not want to fight the Indians; and besides, if my father had been com-

ing after me he would have come long before this. I
don't believe one word of it."

Washakie was of the same opinion as I was.

Then one of Pocatello's Indians said he had just come
from Salt Lake City and many people there had asked
him whether he knew anything about the boy that had
been stolen from the whites. He said that all through the
white men's towns they were getting ready to fight, and
he knew that they were coming to get me.

"I know they are not," I said, "for I have heard my
father say many times that if any of his boys ran away he
should never come home again; besides, my father has
an old Gosiute Indian living with him who knows all
about my running away."

Washakie said that it did not look reasonable to him that
they would wait so long and then come to hunt the
boy, especially at that time of the year.

This made the Pocatello Indians angry. "All right,"
they said; "believe that white boy if you would rather
than believe us; but if you get into a fight with the white
men, you need not ask us to help you."

Washakie said that he was not going to have any
trouble with the whites if he could avoid it.

"No," they said, "you are too big a coward to fight
anything"; and off they strutted as mad as hornets.
As they went out they said to one of our Indians that
they would like to get that little white devil out in the
brush and they would soon have another white, curly-
headed scalp to dance around.

When the council met again that night, they did not
have much to say; they all appeared to be in a deep study.
After a little while Washakie said he thought it would be
a good thing to send some of our Indians to the white
settlements to find out what was going on.

"That is the best thing to do," said old Morogonai; "but who will go?"

"It will not be hard to get men enough to go," said Washakie.

The War Chief said it would be better for the white boy to go himself and end all the trouble; for if his folks were coming after him, that would stop them and settle the dispute. Nearly all of the council agreed with the War Chief.

Washakie asked me what I thought about it. I told him that I did not know the way home and I would not go.

"If the council decides that it is the wisest plan for you to go," said the chief, "we will find a way for you to get home safe." He then asked each member of the council what he thought about it, and all were of the opinion that it was the best thing to do.

Mother talked and cried a great deal. I do not remember all she said, but I know that she begged them to send some one else. Washakie was silent for a long time, then he said that I had better go; that he would send two of his men with me to the nearest white town and then I could get home myself.

"I want you to go home," he said, "and when you get there, tell the truth. Tell your father that you came to us of your own accord; and then if you want to come back, we shall be glad to have you come and live with us always."

"All right," I said, "I will go home if you want me to, but I will not stay there."

How mother did take on! It seemed as if it would break her poor old heart, and Hanabi took it very hard, too. I told them not to feel bad, for I would soon come back.

In a few days, I was to leave, so we began to get ready

for the journey. Hanabi and some other squaws set to work to make my clothes, and they soon had enough to dress me in first-class Indian style. The Indians gave me so many buffalo robes and buckskins that one horse could not carry them; so Washakie said that I might have one of the horses they had captured from the Crows.

When the two Indians that were to go with me said they were ready, we packed up. I had in my pack seven buffalo robes, fifteen large buckskins, and ten pairs of very fine moccasins. It was a bulky load, but not very heavy. Just as I was leaving, the little boys gave me so many arrows that I could not get them all in my quiver.

"She knew me the moment she saw me."

16   HOMEWARD BOUND

WHEN we started to leave the village, how my mother did cry! I tried to comfort her by telling her not to feel bad, for I should soon be back. Little did I think it would be the last time I should see her, for I fully intended to return that fall.

We took plenty of dried meat with us to last us through the trip, and away we went. On the fourth day, at noon, we came to a place on the Bear River about twenty miles north of Brigham City, Utah. We stayed there the rest of the day to give our horses a little rest. The two Indians said that they would go no farther, for I could find the way from there very well.

The next morning they helped me pack my horses and put me on the right trail, telling me not to ride too fast, for I could get to the white settlement long before night.

As I left them I said, "You may look for me back in a few days."

"Don't try to come back this fall," they said, "for it is getting too late to cross the mountains, and we may have a big snow at any time now. It will take you six days to get home from here, and that will make it too late for you to return. You had better stay home this winter. The Indians will be there next summer. You can come back with them."

About noon I came to some warm springs. I thought it would be a good idea to wash my face and hands as I had not done it very often for the past two years. I saw that I had plenty of time, for the sun was high, so I unpacked and staked my horses and went to work to give myself a good scrubbing. I ran my fingers through my hair to get the snarls out, but after all my fussing I could not see that I looked much better.

My hands were like an Indian's and my costume was in the latest Indian fashion. My leggings were trimmed with new red flannel, my shirt was of antelope skins, and my frock of heavy buckskin, smoked to a nice reddish hue, with beads of all colors in wide stripes down the breast and on the shoulders, and fringes all around the bottom that reached nearly to my knees. My cap was made of rawhide, with notches all around the top, and looked like a crosscut saw turned upside down. It came to a peak in front, and mother had put a crown in it with muskrat skin.

After I had scrubbed off all the dirt I could, I packed up and started again. I could see the little town long before I came to it. At the first house I reached a man had just driven up with a load of hay. When I asked him where I could find a place to camp, he told me to stay at his place if I wanted to, that he had plenty of hay, and I was welcome, so I took him at his word. Unpacking my horses I tied them under the shed and fed them. By that time the man came out and said that supper was ready. I told him that I had plenty to eat and would rather not go in.

"Come and eat with me," he insisted, and taking me by the hand, he led me into the house.

The women and children stared at me so hard that I felt uncomfortable. The children would look at me, then turn to one another and laugh.

"I suppose you would like to wash before you eat," said the lady. She gave me some water and soap. It was the first soap I had seen for two years. After I had washed, she told me to sit down at the table.

"Don't you take off your hat when you eat?" the man asked.

"No," I said.

"Will you please take it off here?"

I pulled it off.

They had bread and butter and potatoes and gravy and milk — the first I had seen since I left home. But I was mighty glad when I got away from that table.

I went out and watered my horses and gave them some more hay. By this time it was dark, so I made my bed and turned in. Just as I was getting into bed, I saw this man go down town and pretty soon he came back with three more men. I saw them go into the house. Shortly afterwards he came out and said that the bishop was in the house and would like to have a talk with me. I told him that I did not want to talk; but he kept at me until I got up and went into the house.

The bishop said his name was Nichols, or something like that; then he added, "I see by your dress that you have been with the Indians."

I told him that I had lived with them for a year or two.

He said that he had read in the papers about a little boy running away with the Indians, and he thought I might be that boy.

"Maybe I am," I said.

"To what tribe do you belong?"

"Washakie's tribe."

"I have heard," he said, "that Washakie is a chief among the Shoshones and that his tribe is friendly to the white people. What do you know about them?"

"Washakie's band," I replied, "are good Indians. I have heard the chief say many times that he was a friend to the people of Utah, that he had seen their big chief, who was a very good 'tibo.'"

"What is that?" he asked.

"Oh, I forgot I was talking to white men," I said; "'tibo' means friend."

I told them that he had no need to fear Washakie's tribe, but that old Pocatello had drawn away some of Washakie's Indians, and that they were bad Indians, who were doing everything against the whites they could. Washakie had told me they were killing the emigrants and stealing their horses and burning their wagons.

Well, this bishop talked and talked, and asked me ten thousand questions, it seemed to me. Finally the woman took pity on me and said, "Do let the poor boy rest."

I told them I had always been in bed by dark and that I felt pretty tired.

"Well," said the bishop, "you may go to bed now, and I will see you in the morning. You had better come down to my house and stay all day. I should like very much to have Brother Snow talk with you."

I didn't say anything, but I thought that neither Snow nor rain would catch me in that place another day, so I was up by the peep of day and away I went. I traveled seven or eight miles and stopped by some hot springs, unpacked my horses, and got me something to eat. I thought that I would not stop in any more houses where bishops could get hold of me and talk me to death.

After my horses had fed, I started on my way again, and after traveling about ten miles more, I came to a place called Ogden. As I was going along the main street, a man standing by a store stopped me and began talking Indian to me. He asked me where I had been. I told him. While we were talking, several more men came up and one of them asked me where I was going to camp that night. I told him that I did not know, but that I would go on down the road a piece until I found grass and water. He asked me to put my horses in his corral and give them all the hay they could eat.

"No," I said, "I would rather go on."

"No," he said, "you must stop here tonight." With that he took the rope out of my hands and let my horses into his corral. I followed him, and when I had unpacked I asked him if he was a bishop. He said he was. I told him I thought so.

"Why?" he asked.

"Because you talk so much."

He laughed and said that I must not mind that, for they seldom saw a person like me, and they wanted to find out all they could about the Indians.

After a while he invited me in to supper. I did not want to go, but he would have his way, so I went in with him. I think he said his name was West.

This Bishop West, if that was his name, asked me a good many questions, but he said he would not weary me by talking too long. I was in bed soon after dark that night. I intended to get off early the next morning, and give them the slip as before ; but just as I was packing up, the bishop came out and said, "Hold on there, you are not going before breakfast."

I told him that I had plenty to eat with me ; but he insisted that I take breakfast with him, and I had to stay.

Jordan River and Wasatch Mountains, Salt Lake Valley, Utah. The Pony Express and Overland Stage road ran through this valley.

He asked me a great many more questions, but he was very nice about it. I felt glad to talk with him, for he was so kind and good to me.

He said that I would be a very useful man, if I was treated right. He asked me whether I had been to school much, and he was very much surprised when I told him that I had never attended school a day in my life. He said that I must go to school, and if I lived near him he would see that I did go. As I started away he asked me to go and see Governor Young when I got to Salt Lake; but I thought I did not want to do it. I was a young boy then and did not realize the importance of his request.

That day I reached a place called Farmington. Just as I was nearing town, I saw some boys driving cows.

"Where can I camp tonight?" I asked them.

"Up on the mountain if you want to," said one of them.

"You think you are pretty smart," I said.

"Just as smart as you, Mr. Injun," he replied; "if you don't believe it, just get off that buzzard head of a horse and I'll show you."

I jumped off and he ran. I got on my horse and started after them, but they scrambled through the fence and ran away through the fields. I went on through the town, and after getting permission from the owner, camped in his field, and I was not bothered with any questions that night.

The next morning I was off pretty early and reached Salt Lake City. I did not stay there, however, but went on through and stopped at the Jordan River bridge for noon. This was a familiar road to me now, for I had been in the city several times before. That afternoon I journeyed on to what we called Black Rock and camped that night at the southern end of Great Salt Lake. I was now

within a short day's ride of home. I could hardly stay
there till morning, I was so anxious now to get home.

Just as I was making camp, a team drove up with three
people in the wagon. I knew them. They were John
Zundel, his sister Julia, and Jane Branden, our nearest
neighbors, but they did not know me at first.

I had a fire and was broiling a rabbit I had killed, when
Julia came up and tried to get a good look at me, but I
kept my face turned from her as much as I could. Finally
she got a glimpse of my face and went to the wagon. I
heard her say to Jane,

"That is the whitest Indian I ever saw, and he has blue
eyes."

"I'll bet a dollar it is Nick Wilson," said Jane.

They came over where I was and Jane said, "Look up
here, young man, and let us see you."

I let them take a look at me.

"I knew it was you, you little scamp!" she said, taking hold of me and shaking me and patting me on the
back.

"I've a good notion to flog you," she went on. "Your
poor mother has worried herself nearly to death about
you."

Morning came at last, and I packed up in a hurry to get
home. I did not stop this time until I reached it.

As I rode up, two of my little sisters, who were playing
by the side of the house, ran in and told mother that an
Indian was out there. She came to the door, and she
knew me the moment she saw me. I cannot tell you just
what passed the next hour, but they were all happy to
have me back safe at home again.

I had forgotten all about my horses in the joy of the
meeting. When I finally went out to unpack them, the
folks all followed me and mother asked, "Where did you

get all of those horses? Did you take them from the Indians and run away?"

I told her that they were mine, that I had not run away from the Indians as I had from her. After that I put my ponies in the field, and answering their eager questions, I told them all about my two years among the Indians.

17 THE YEAR OF THE MOVE

Soon after I reached home, another call was made for men to go out and stop the soldiers from entering the territory. I wanted to go, but my father would not let me. I said that I could shoot as well with my bow and arrows as they could with their old flintlock guns, but they said I was too young, so my older brother went, and I let him have one of my buffalo robes and my roan pony.

All of the grain was not out of the fields yet and all of the men had gone off to the "Echo Canyon War," as it was called, except a few very old men who could not do much work. The women and little boys could be seen every day out in the fields hauling grain and stacking it. There would be about half a dozen women to each team and a little boy driving the oxen. I have seen as many as fifteen to twenty teams at a time out in the big public field hauling grain, and just as many women and children as could get around the wagons. They seemed happy as larks, for they were singing bravely.

After the grain was hauled it was threshed. An old man by the name of Baker, who could just get around by the aid of two walking-sticks, took charge of the threshing machine. It was not much like the steam threshers of these days. This one had a cylinder fixed in a big box, and it was made to turn by horse power, but we had to use ox power. Old "Daddy Baker" and as many women as could get around the machine began to do the threshing. We put on four yoke of oxen to run the old "chaff-piler," as we called it.

The oldest boys were set to pitching the grain to the old machine. One of the other boys started up the cattle and away she went. I was to do the feeding. At first the boys pitched the grain so fast that I had to shove three or four bundles at a time into the mouth of the machine. This choked the old thing, and caused the belt to break, and it took half an hour to patch up and get going again.

The straw and chaff came out together. About fifteen women with rakes would string out and rake the straw along until they left the grain behind, then about forty children would stack the straw. After we threshed an hour or two we would stop and "cave up," as we called it. That meant to push the grain and chaff in a pile at one side. Then we would go on again.

When we had finished Brother Martendale's job, we moved over to Brother Pumpswoggle's place, and after that we threshed for some other brother until all the grain was done.

After the threshing was done, we took the old-fashioned fanning mill and went the rounds to clean the chaff from the grain. Some of the women would take turns turning the old thing, while others would take milk pans and buckets and put grain into the hopper. The chaff would ny one way and the grain go another. At best we could thresh only about one hundred fifty bushels a day, and we had about twenty thousand bushels to thresh, so it looked a very discouraging task, with winter so near.

But as luck would have it, some of the men came in with a large band of mules and horses they had taken from the soldiers and four of the men were left home to help do the threshing. "Lonzo" Mecham took charge of the work, and we used some of the captured mules to help out, so the threshing went on much faster. They were good mules.

During all of that fall the women took the part of men as well as women. They hauled wood from the mountains, dug potatoes, and gathered in all of the other products from the gardens and farms. Many of the poor mothers were hardly able to be out, but they took their double part bravely while their fathers, brothers and sons were off in the mountains defending their homes and families. They were poorly dressed, too, for the cold weather.

Most of the people were very poor. The Indians and grasshoppers and crickets had kept them down so that it was hard at best to make a living, and now an army was coming, they feared, to burn and kill.

The soldiers probably would have made sad work, if Lot Smith had not stopped them by burning their wagon trains full of supplies out on the Big Sandy.[1] This held them off long enough to enable the officers of the government to meet with the leaders of the state and come to an understanding; the war was happily prevented.

During the winter many of the men came home. Poor though we were we had happy times. They had social gatherings at which they sang and danced and played games to while away the wintry evenings. Sometimes,

[1] A branch of the Green River, in Wyoming.

Echo Canyon, Utah. The Overland Trail ran through this pass.

to pay the fiddler, the people took squash or wheat or carrots. There was little money in the country.

I have said that the people were very poor. They were poor in furniture, bedding, clothing, but generally they had enough to eat, and they were gradually getting cattle, sheep, pigs, and chickens to help out. Their furniture and dishes, however, had been broken and used up in their long journey across the plains and it was hard to get more. Sometimes a coat or a dress would be patched so many times and with so many different kinds of cloth that it was difficult to tell which piece of cloth it had been made of in the first place.

When spring came, matters had not been yet arranged between our leaders and the government. The leaders were uncertain how the trouble would end, so they ordered the settlers to abandon their homes for the time being and move south. This was a trying thing to do. The crops were all in when the order came to move. A guard was left to take care of what was left behind, and if it came to the worst, they were to burn everything that might be useful to the army. My father with his family and most of our neighbors moved down to Spanish Fork, Utah. Here we stayed for further orders from the authorities.

To make this move from their homes, the people had to use any kind of outfit they could get together. Everything from a wheelbarrow to an eight-mule team could be seen along the roads. An old wagon with a cow and a horse hitched up together was a common sight. Some had good buggies, others an old ox hitched between the shafts of a rickety old two-wheeled cart. Some of the women led the family cows with their bedding and a little food packed on their backs. Some were rich and many were poor, but they all were traveling the same road, and all appeared to be happy, and none of them very badly scared.

By this time I had traded my Crow Indian pony for a white man's saddle and a two-year-old heifer. I wanted to go back to live with Washakie and my dear old Indian mother, but I did not care to do so until I found out what the army was going to do.

We had not been in Spanish Fork long before some Spaniards from California brought in a band of wild horses to trade for cattle. A good many people had

Remains of levee built by Utah troops to flood a canyon
so as to impede the march of Johnston's army.

gathered around the corral to see the mustangs. While
sitting on the corral fence, I saw a little black three-
year-old mare that took my fancy. I asked the man
what he would take for her.

"She is worth sixty dollars," he said, "but if you will

jump off that fence on to her back and ride her, you may have her for nothing."

"That is a whack," I said; "I'll do it."

He told me to wait until they were ready to turn the horses out. It was not long before he said, "Now we are ready to see the fun." He had no idea that I would do it. He thought the colt would throw me off at the first jump, and they would have a good laugh on my account.

They let down the bars and drove the horses around so that the black came near enough for me to jump off the fence to her back. As she came close I made the leap and landed fairly. Away she went out through the bars and down the street. Every dog in the place seemed to be after us.

We passed over the hill and headed towards Pond Town. Then we circled to the west towards Goshen. The band of horses we started with were soon left way behind and we ran away from all the dogs.

Some one ran over and told my folks that I was on a wild horse, that it was running away and I would be killed. Mother was not much worried, for she knew I had been on wild horses before. My brother, however, jumped on my pinto pony and struck out after me. When he finally caught up, the colt I had been riding had run herself down, and had stopped. He rode up and handed me a rope, which I put around the mare's neck, and then got off to let her rest. After a while I mounted her again and with my brother drove her back to town. The stranger kept his word. I had won the black mare.

When we got back, all of the men that had seen us start off came up to look at us. Among them was a Mr. Faust, "Doc Faust," they called him. He said that I beat all the boys at riding he ever saw ; that he had a good many horses on his ranch he wanted broken and would give me fifty dollars a month to come and do it for him. When I told mother about it, she would not give her consent, for my father was very sick and she was afraid he would not live much longer.

We stayed in the neighborhood of Spanish Fork until about the first of August, then word came that we could go back home. The leaders had come to a peaceful agreement with the government.

We started back to our homes with a hurrah ! and when we reached them, we all went to work with a will. I never saw larger crops than we raised that year. Wheat ran from fifty to seventy-five bushels to the acre. It was the same all through the territory. Best of all we received the highest prices for it. The army bought all the grain, hay, straw, and other products that we had to sell.

All of our harvesting had to be done by hand, for there were no reaping machines in those days. We hired Owen Baston to cradle our grain, and my brother and I bound it. That fall, after our wheat was all harvested, my father died.

After the death of father, my brother and I did not get along very well together. He was a hard worker. I had never done much work and it went rather hard with me. Riding horses, I thought, was more fun than slaving on the farm, so I decided to go to Mr. Faust's ranch and help him break his bronchos. After that I intended to go back to live with Washakie.

Mr. Faust lived at the south end of Rush Valley, about sixty miles southwest of Salt Lake. When I got to his ranch he was very glad to see me.

"We will have that old outlaw of a horse brought to

time now," he said to his other riders. "Here is the boy that can ride him."

I told him that I was not so sure of that, for I had never ridden a bad horse for more than a year.

"Bad," he said, "what do you call jumping off a fence on to the back of a wild mustang?"

"Oh, she wasn't a bad animal to ride," I said; "she did nothing but run."

"My horses are not bad to break," he went on, "but one of them has thrown two or three of the boys, and it has made him mean. I want him broken, for he is about as good a horse as I have, and I know you can break him."

The next morning one of Mr. Faust's best riders and I went out to bring in the band the outlaw was with. This man told me that if I was not a very good rider I had better keep off that horse, or he would kill me. I told him that I did not know much about riding, but I was not afraid to try him. We brought in the band and roped the outlaw.

Part of fortifications built by Utah troops to hold back Johnston's army.

Mr. Faust asked me whether I thought I could ride him. I was ready to try. The man who had gone with me tried to get Mr. Faust not to let me do it, for he said I might be killed. I began to think he was afraid I should prove the better rider, for the outlaw had pitched him off several times.

When things were ready, I mounted the broncho. He went off very peaceably for a little way, and I thought that they were making a fool of me; but pretty soon the old boy turned loose, and he fairly made my neck pop. He gave me the hardest bucking I ever had; but he did it straight ahead. He did not whirl as some horses do, so I stayed with him all right.

When he stopped bucking, I sent him through for ten miles about as fast as he ever went, and when I got back to the ranch I rode up the corral where the man was saddling another horse.

Standing up in my saddle, I said, "Do you call this a bad horse? If you do you don't know what a bad horse is."

The fellow did not like me very much after that. I got along very well with the old outlaw; but I had to give him some very hard rides before he acknowledged me his master.

I had a number of similar experiences in taming horses which were hard to manage, and although I did not come out without a scratch or a bruise, I succeeded in making almost any horse I tried to ride understand that I was his master. However, I would not advise a boy who has not a particular faculty for riding unmanageable horses to engage in the sport on the strength of my remarks here. It takes quite a knack to establish the right understanding between a horse and a man. Some persons — women as well as men — seem to have this gift naturally, and without any idea of boasting I may say that I think I had it more than most of the boys in our part of the country.

One reason, perhaps, why I got along so well with them was that ever since I was a little boy I have loved horses and liked to be around them, thinking of them more as human beings than mere dumb beasts. It was the same way, I may add, with dogs; and horses and dogs know when a boy or a man has this feeling, and it makes a difference even in the toughest of them as to how they will treat you.

I am sorry that I cannot stop and make it a part of my story to tell about some more of my adventures in taming wild horses. But possibly this is just as well, as I am afraid true stories might not prove very interesting beside some which have been printed in papers and magazines, in which I think the writers must have drawn largely upon their imagination in order to make thrilling "yarns."

18   THE PONY EXPRESS

ABOUT the time I had decided to go back to my Indian
friends, word came that the Pony Express was to be
started, and Mr. Faust induced me to stay and be one
of the pony riders.   I sold my roan pony to a sergeant
in Camp Floyd for seventy-five dollars and my little
black mare for a hundred dollars.   Part of this money
I gave to mother, and the rest I used to buy some clothes.

A great "powwow" was going on about the Pony
Express coming through the country.   The company
had begun to build its roads and stations.   These stations
were about ten miles apart.   They were placed as near
to a spring, or other watering place, as possible.   There
were two kinds of them, the "home station" and the
"way station."   At the way stations, the riders changed
horses; at the home stations, which were about fifty
miles from each other, the riders were changed; and
there they ate their meals and slept.

Finally the time came for the express horses to be
distributed along the line, and the station keepers and

riders were sent to the various stations. Mr. Faust and Major Howard Egan went on my bond, and I was sent out west into Nevada to a station called Ruby Valley. This was a "home station." It was kept by William Smith. Samuel Lee was his hostler.

When we were hired to ride the express, we had to go before a justice of the peace and swear we would be at our post at all times, and not go farther than one hundred yards from the station except when carrying the mail. When we started out we were not to turn back, no matter what happened, until we had delivered the mail at the next station. We must be ready to start back at a half minute's notice, day or night, rain or shine, Indians or no Indians.

Our saddles, which were all provided by the company, had nothing to them but the bare tree, stirrups, and cinch. Two large pieces of leather about sixteen inches wide by twenty-four long were laced together with a strong leather string thrown over the saddle. Fastened to these were four pockets, two in front and two behind; these hung on each side of the saddle. The two hind ones were the largest. The one in front on the left side was called the "way pocket." All of these pockets were locked with small padlocks and each home station keeper had a key to the "way pocket." When the express arrived at the home station, the keeper would unlock the "way pocket" and if there were any letters for the boys between the home stations, the rider would distribute them as he went along. There was also a card in the way pocket that the station keeper would take out and write on it the time the express arrived and left his station. If the express was behind time, he would tell the rider how much time he had to make up.

Well, the time came that we had to start. On the afternoon of April 3, 1860, at a signal cannon shot, a pony rider left St. Joseph, Missouri; and the same moment another left Sacramento, California — one speeding west, the other east over plains and mountains and desert. Night and day the race was kept up by the different riders and their swift horses until the mail was carried through. Then they turned and dashed back over the same trail again. Each man would make about fifty miles a day, changing horses four or five times to do it.

Not many riders could stand the long, fast riding at first, but after about two weeks they would get hardened to it.

At first the rider would be charged up with the saddle he was riding, and his first wages were kept back for it. If he had no revolver, and had to get one from the company, that would add another heavy expense to be deducted from his wages. Some of the boys were killed by the Indians before they had paid for these things. Our pay was too small for the hard work and the dangers we went through.

Everything went along first rate for a while, but after about six or eight months of that work, the big, fine horses began to play out, and then the company bought up a lot of wild horses from California, strung them along the road and put the best riders to breaking them.

Peter Neece, our home station keeper, was a big, strong man, and a good rider. He was put to breaking some of these mustangs for the boys on his beat. After he had ridden one of them a time or two, he would turn the half-broken, wild things over to the express boys to ride. Generally, when a hostler could lead them into and out of the stable without getting his head kicked off, the bronchos were considered broken. Very likely they had been handled just enough to make them mean. I found it to be so with most of the horses they gave me to ride.

I was not a bit afraid of the Indians at first; but when the boys began to get shot at and killed by the skulking savages, I might not have been afraid, but I was pretty badly scared just the same.

At one time my home station was at Shell Creek. I rode from there to Deep Creek. One day the Indians killed a rider out on the desert, and when I was to meet him at Deep Creek, he was not there. I had to keep right on until I met him. It was not until I reached the next station, Willow Creek, that I found out he had been killed. My horse was about jaded by this time, so I had to stay there and let him rest. I should have had to start back that night if the Indians had not come upon us.

About four o'clock that afternoon, seven Indians rode up to the station and asked for something to eat. Neece, the station keeper, picked up a sack holding about twenty pounds of flour and offered it to them. They demanded a sack of flour apiece. He threw it back into the house and told them to clear out, that he would not give them anything.

This made them angry, and as they passed a shed about five rods from the house they each shot an arrow into a poor old lame cow, that happened to be standing under a shed. When Neece saw that, he jerked out his pistol and commenced shooting at them. He killed two of the Indians and the rest ran.

"Now, boys," he said, "we are in for a hot time tonight. There's a bunch of about thirty of the red rascals up the canyon, and they will be on us as soon as it gets dark. We'll have to fight."

A man by the name of Lynch was with us at the time. He had boasted a good deal about what he would do if the Indians attacked him. We thought he was a kind of desperado. I felt pretty safe until he weakened and began to cry, then I wanted all of us to get on our horses and skip for the next station; but Pete said: "No; we will load up all of our old guns and get ready for them when they come. There are only four of us; but we can stand off the whole bunch of them."

Just a little before dark we could see a big dust over towards the mouth of the canyon about six miles from the station. We knew they were coming. Neece

Bur. of Am. Ethnology, Smithsonian Institution

An aged Indian of the Nevada desert, of Pony Express days, with his bow and arrows.

thought it would be a good thing to go out from the station a hundred yards or so and surprise them as they came up. When we got there he had us lie down a little way apart.

"Now," he said, "when you fire, jump to one side, so if they shoot at the blaze of your gun, you will not be there."

You bet I lay close to the ground. Pretty soon we heard the thumping of their horses' hoofs. It seemed to me there were hundreds of them. And such yells as they let out, I never heard before. They were coming straight for us, and I thought they were going to run right over us. It was sandy where we lay, with little humps here and there and scrubby greasewood growing on the humps.

When the Indians got close enough, Pete shot and jumped away to one side. I had two pistols, one in each hand, cocked and ready to pull the trigger, and was crawling on my elbows and knees. Each time he would shoot I saw him jump. Soon they were all shooting but me I got so excited that I forgot to fire, but I kept jumping.

After I had jumped a good many times, I happened to land in a little wash, or ravine, that the water had made. My back came up nearly level with the top of the banks. Anyway I pressed myself down in it. I was badly scared. My heart was beating like a triphammer.

As I lay there, the shooting ceased. After a while I raised my head and looked off towards the desert. Those humps of sand covered with greasewood looked exactly like Indians on horses, and I could see several of them near the wash. I crouched down again and lay there a long time; it seemed hours.

Finally everything was so still I decided to go and see whether my horse was where I had staked him. If he was, I intended to jump on him and strike back for the Deep Creek station, and tell them that the boys were killed; but as I went crawling around the house on my elbows and knees with my revolvers ready to shoot, I saw a light shining through the cracks. It must be full of Indians, I thought; and I lay there quietly to watch what they were doing.

Suddenly I heard one of the men a little distance from the house say, "Did you find anything of him?"

Another answered: "No, I guess he is gone."

I knew then it was the boys. When I heard them go into the house and shut the door, I slipped up and peeped through the cracks. The three of them were in there all right. I was almost too ashamed to go in; but I finally went around and opened the door.

"Hello!" Neece called out; "here he is! How far did you chase them, Nick? I knew you would stay with them."

Several Indians had been killed and the rest of the bunch had run when the surprise attack was made on them. They did not bother us any more just then, but they got plenty of revenge later. The next morning I went back to Deep Creek.

Shortly after this I was making my ride through one of the canyons on the trail when suddenly four Indians jumped out of the rocks and brush into the road just ahead of me. I whirled my pony and started to run back, when I found three other Indians standing in the trail. I couldn't climb the sides of the canyon; the devils had me trapped, and they began to close in on me with their bows and arrows ready. Only one of them had a gun.

I did not know what else to do, so I sat still on my horse. As they came up I recognized old Tabby among them. This gave me some hope. Their leader, a one-eyed, mean-looking old rascal, grabbed my horse's rein, and ordered me to get off. I tried to get old Tabby's eye, but he wouldn't look my way nor speak to me. Two Indians led my horse about a hundred yards up the canyon and held it there, while the one-eyed Indian talked to me.

He said I had no right to cross their country. The land belonged to the Indians, and they were going to drive the white men out of it. He took his ramrod out of his old gun and marked a trail in the road. "We will burn the stations, here and here and here," he went on, jabbing the rod in the dirt. "And we will kill the pony men."

With this threat he left me standing in the road, while

"Joe Dugout's" well on old Pony Express trail, about ten miles north-east of Camp Floyd. "Joe" kept a "way station" here for the express.

he, with old Tabby and the rest, walked away into the brush and began to talk. I could not hear what they were saying. I was badly scared. Then they made a fire.

My soul! I thought. Are they going to burn me? I was just about to make a dash for the two Indians and fight for my horse; but that would have been a fool thing to do.

After a while one of the Indians came up and asked me if I had any tobacco. I gave him all I had. That made things look a little better. They had a smoke and then Old Tabby came to talk with me.

The Indians, he said, wanted to kill me, but he would not agree to it. My father, he said, was his good friend. But I must turn back and never carry the mail there again; for if they caught me they would surely kill me next time.

"But this mail's got to go through," I said. "Let me take it this time and I will not ride here again."

When I had made this promise, they let me go. I did not carry the mail over there any more; but I was sent further west, about three hundred miles, to ride from Carson Sink to Fort Churchill. The distance was about seventy-five miles and was a very hard ride, for the horses as well as for me, because much of the trail led through deep sand. Some things were not so bad, however; I had no mountains to cross, and the Indians were more friendly here.

East of my beat along Egan Canyon, Shell Creek, and Deep Creek, they had begun to be very ugly, threatening to burn the stations and kill the people, and the following spring they did break out in dead earnest. Some of the stations were burned and one of the riders was killed. That spring I was changed back into Major Egan's division and rode from Shell Creek to Ruby Valley.

Things grew worse that summer. More stations were burned, some hostlers and riders were killed, and I got very badly wounded. It happened this way. I had been taking some horses to Antelope Station, and on my way back, I made a stop at Spring Valley Station. When I got there, the two boys that looked after the station were out on the wood pile playing cards. They asked me to stay and have dinner. I got my horse and started him towards the station, but instead of going into the stable he went behind it where some other horses were grazing.

Pretty soon we saw the horses going across the meadow towards the cedars with two Indians behind them. We started after them full tilt and gained on them a little. As we ran I fired three shots at them from my revolver, but they were too far off for me to hit them. They reached the cedars a little before we did.

I was ahead of the other two boys, and as I ran around a large cedar one of the Indians shot me in the head with a flint-tipped arrow. It struck me about two inches above the left eye. The two boys were on the other side of the tree. Seeing the Indians run, they came around to find me lying on the ground with the arrow sticking in my head. They tried to pull the arrow out, but the shaft came away and left the flint in my head. Thinking that I would surely die, they rolled me under a tree and started for the next station as fast as they could go. There they got a few men and came back the next morning to bury me; but when they got to me and found that I was still alive, they thought they would not bury me just then.

They carried me to a station called Cedar Wells, and sent to Ruby Valley for a doctor. When he came, he took the spike out of my head and told the boys to keep a wet rag on the wound, as that was all they could do for me.

I lay there for six days, when Major Egan happened to come along. Seeing that I was still alive, he sent for the doctor again. When the doctor came and saw I was no worse, he began to do something for me. But I knew nothing of all this. For eighteen days I lay unconscious. Then I began to get better fast, and it was not long before I was riding again.

If Mr. Egan had not happened along when he did, I think I should not be here now telling about it. But oh, I have suffered with my head at times since then!

The Indians kept getting worse. They began to attack and murder emigrants, and they did a lot of damage to the express line by burning stations, killing the riders, and running off with the horses. It became harder to get riders to carry the mail; for every one that could leave would do so, and the agents found it difficult to find others to take the dangerous job. They raised the wages from forty dollars to sixty per month, but men did not want to risk their lives for even that price.

Between Deep Creek and Shell Creek was what we called "Eight-mile station." It was kept by an old man, and he had two young emigrant boys to help him. Their mother had died of the cholera, east of Salt Lake City, and their father had been shot by the Indians farther along the trail west. He died when they reached Deep Creek, leaving these two boys with the station keeper. Before he passed away he gave this keeper five hundred dollars, a span of big mules, and a new wagon if he would send the boys back to Missouri where the family had lived.

As it was too late for them to make the trip that fall, the boys were to pass the winter at Deep Creek. The old keeper of the "Eight-mile station" could not do the work very well, so the older of the two boys was sent there to help him. An emigrant train came along and the old man slipped away with it, leaving the boy to take care of the station alone. It was hard to get men to stay at this station when the Indians began to get mean. The boy wanted to stay with it, so they let him do it; and his brother was sent out to help him.

One day, while these two boys were in charge, I rode up there to meet the other rider. As I reached the station, I could see him coming five or six miles away. While we were watching him a band of Indians broke out of the brush and began to chase him. He made a great race for his life; but just before he reached the station, they shot and killed him. We knew the Indians would attack the station next, so we hurried to the barn and brought the three horses there to the house.

The station was a stone building about twelve by twenty feet in size, with a shed roof covered with dirt, so that no timbers were sticking out for the Indians to set on fire. There were portholes in each end of the building, and one on each side of the door in front.

We succeeded in getting our horses into this house by the time the Indians surrounded the station. They kept shooting at the back of the house; for they soon learned not to come up in front of these portholes. One or two of them that were foolish enough to do it got killed. I know that one made a mistake by darkening my porthole. When I saw the shadow, I pulled the trigger. Three days afterwards, when I went out, I found an Indian lying there. He must have got in the way of my bullet.

They kept us there for three days. It was lucky for us that the station was built on low ground. The water had risen in the cellar under the house. We had only one pan that the boys had used for mixing dough to make their bread. This we had to use to water and feed the horses in and for mixing bread also. The water in the cellar was not good, but it kept us from choking to death those three days that we were held prisoners.

The younger boy was not more than eleven years old, and the other one was about fourteen. I was only a few years older. We put the little boy to tending the horses and looking after things while we guarded the house. Sometimes the little fellow would get to crying, and talking about his mother dying and his father getting killed by the Indians. The older boy was full of grit. He would try to comfort his little brother.

The first night none of us slept at all, but the next day and the following night I let them sleep a little by having one of them watch while the other slept. The third night I went to sleep and left the boys on guard.

Along towards morning, just as it was getting daylight, they came and woke me up. There was a lot of shooting going on outside, and they wanted to know what it meant. I listened, and the first thing I heard was somebody say-

ing, "Go to the house and see if the boy is all right." I looked through the hole and saw a lot of soldiers. Some of Johnston's army had been sent out to clear the trail of the murdering Indians.

Another exciting experience happened to me when Mr. Kennedy, a horse trader, was bringing a large band of mustangs along the trail from California to Salt Lake to sell. He got belated out on the desert and found it necessary to stop at Deep Creek, where he could winter his horses out instead of feeding them. The Indians were so bad that we had to send out guards with the horses in the daytime, and at night corral them, and place a strong guard around them.

Our corral was made by digging a trench and setting in large cedar posts on end. There was a straw stack in the middle of the corral where the boys tried to sleep; but the Indians got so mean that they would shoot arrows in the bed. This made it too dangerous to sleep there. Sometimes we would spread our blankets on the straw as if we were in bed, and in the morning find several arrows sticking through them.

A favorite way of guarding the corral was to take up a big picket, or post on either side of the bars, and have a man stand in its place.

The Indians' scheme was to get the bars down in some way, then stampede the horses, and run them off. One night Peter Neece and I were standing guard in this way. He was on one side of the bars and I was on the other. We knew that there were Indians around by the way the horses in the corral acted. I was standing on the south side of the bars looking off into the sagebrush, for I believed the Indians would be coming from that direction, because the horses were looking that way.

But one Indian, instead of coming straight up from the

front, got close up to the fence at the back and came creeping around close to the corral to get to the bars. It happened that he was coming on my side, but I did not see him. Neece did, but he could not warn me without giving himself away.

He watched him crawling towards the bars, and just as he got about to his feet, Neece fired. The Indian gave one unearthly yell that could have been heard for miles, sprang in the air and settled down where I had been standing, but I wasn't there. When that yell was being let out, I turned a back somersault and landed a rod or more inside of the corral.

Sometimes at night when the horses were brought in, we would saddle one for each of us and keep him saddled ready for use all night. In the morning we would put the saddle on fresh horses to be prepared at any minute to strike out after the Indians if it was necessary.

In the spring, when Mr. Kennedy was about to start with his horses for Salt Lake, the herder was fired on one morning as he was driving the band out to grass. The Indians then closed in behind the horses and headed them towards the hills. Seven of us immediately started after them. I was on a lazy, old blue horse, and could not keep up with the other boys, but Mr. Kennedy rode a very good horse. He was way ahead of the rest of us and was crowding the Indians pretty close. He would have overtaken them in a few minutes more. Just before he caught up with them, however, one Indian's horse fell, carrying his rider down with him. As Kennedy charged on the Indian to run over him, he received an arrow in the arm; but the Indian got a bullet through the head in return. Kennedy had to wait until we came up to pull the arrow out of his arm.

By that time the Indians had the horses in a box canyon

A coyote, an animal often seen on the desert, along the Pony Express trail. See Mark Twain's description of the coyote, in *Roughing It.*

A few of the thieves hid among the rocks and held us back while the rest of the band rushed the horses up the canyon. The canyon led south a few hundred yards, then turned sharply around a large, steep mountain and ran almost directly north. A short distance further the canyon turned again and opened into a large meadow about a mile long.

When we saw that we could not pass the Indians that were ambushing us at the rocky entrance of the canyon, Kennedy thought it would be best to go back two or three miles and cross a low divide to get into it at the head of the meadow. There the canyon narrowed again. We might head off the Indians if we got there first. We turned and went back about two and a half miles to go over this divide. When we neared the top of the divide there was a cliff too steep to take our horses over, so we tied them to a clump of mountain mahogany, and went afoot. We could not go very fast down the other side, for the white maple brush was very thick.

Just before we got down to the head of the meadows, we stopped on the side of the mountain near a very large flat-topped rock. Kennedy sat there watching for the Indians to come out on to the meadows from the canyon. The rest of us went down just below the rock and began to fill our pockets with "yarb," or Indian tobacco. While picking this "yarb," Frank Mathis laid his old muzzle-loading Springfield rifle down in the bushes where he could easily reach it if necessary.

We had been there about half an hour when all at once Kennedy jumped down among us and cried, "Boys, we're surrounded!" In his excitement Mathis grabbed his gun by the muzzle and gave it a jerk. The hammer caught on a bush and the gun was discharged, shooting his left arm off between the shoulder and elbow. That rattled us a good deal so we hardly knew what to do next.

Kennedy thought it best for us to fight our way back to where our horses were tied. He started Mathis up the hill ahead of the rest of us. We were to keep the Indians back if we could. We knew they were around us on every side for we could hear the brush cracking and see it shaking every once in a while. When near the top, we came to a bare stretch of ground about two rods across.

We stopped at the edge of the brush, for we knew that the Indians could shoot us as soon as we got into the open. Kennedy thought we had better make a break for it and scatter out as we ran so that they could not hit us so easily. I had the shortest legs of all the men ; but, just the same, I wasn't the last one over. When we were about half way across, the Indians opened fire with their bows and guns. One bullet struck a rock right under my feet. It helped me over the hill just that much quicker.

By the time we reached the horses, Mathis was bleeding badly. He was faint and begging for water. We had to lead our horses down to the bottom of the mountain on account of the rocks. Kennedy sent Robert Orr and me down to the creek to get water in our hats for Mathis. When we got back with it, Kennedy sent me on to the station so I could be there when the express came and be ready to take it on. That was the last I ever saw of Frank Mathis. He was sent on to Salt Lake, where he was cared for and got well, but he got into trouble later and was killed.

About the time the Indians were at their worst a small train of emigrants came through on their way to California. They were warned by all of the station agents that it was not safe for so few people to travel through the country at that time, and were advised to stop until more trains came up. They replied that they were well armed and could stand off the Indians all right.

At that time I was riding from Shell Creek through Egan Canyon to Ruby Valley. We who knew the Gosiute Indians could tell that they were going to make a raid. They were making signals in the mountains with smokes by day and fires by night to gather their band. We knew by their signs that the emigrants would be attacked as they were going through some of the bad canyons on the route. Egan Canyon was about the worst of these; it was a narrow canyon nearly six miles long, with cliffs on each side from three hundred to one thousand feet high, so that one could not turn to the right or the left after entering it. This canyon was the dread of all that had to go through it.

The train of emigrants had entered this canyon just ahead of me. I rode very fast to catch up with them before they got to the worst part of it, but just before I reached them, I heard the shooting and I knew the Indians had made an attack. As I stopped to listen two men came running for dear life. They were bareheaded.

"Go back!" they shouted as they came near, "The whole company has been killed but us." They passed me and ran on.

After a little while I could hear no more shooting, so I went on cautiously, looking ahead and around at every turn of the road. Soon I came in sight of the wagons. I made sure the Indians had gone before I went up to them.

Such a terrible sight I never saw before. Every man, woman, and child except the two that escaped had been cruelly murdered. Only one woman had any life left when I got there and she died a moment later. I looked around carefully to see whether any others were alive, but finding none I rode on. I could not stand to look long on the dreadful scene. The Indians had cut the tugs of the harnesses and taken every horse and mule in the train. When I got out of the canyon, and saw where the murderous band had turned off the road, I did not spare my horse until I reached the next station. The keeper there immediately sent a messenger to Ruby Valley where the soldiers were and they came and buried the unfortunate emigrants.

19   JOHNSTON PUNISHES THE INDIANS

THE Indians became so troublesome that the soldiers from
Camp Floyd were called out to stop their dreadful work.
I got a letter from Major Egan directing me to meet him
at Camp Floyd as soon as I could get there, for they
wanted me to act as interpreter and guide for the soldiers.
I started at once and made two hundred miles in three
days. When I reached Camp Floyd, General Albert
Sidney Johnston was all ready to start out against the
Indians with four companies of soldiers. We traveled
west, and crossed the Great American Desert in the night,
so as not to be seen by the Indians.

The soldiers stayed at Fish Springs and sent me out with
three other scouts to see if we could find any signs of the
Indians we were after. We took only two days' rations
with us. The first day we met with no success, so the next
morning we separated. I sent two of the scouts to circle
around to the south, and took with me a young man by the
name of Johnson, and went northwest. That afternoon
we saw two Indians crossing a valley. We kept out of

sight but followed them until night, and saw them go into a small bunch of cedars. We left our horses and slipped up as close to them as we could without letting them see us.

When we got pretty near to them, I recognized in one of the Indians my old friend Yaiabi; but not feeling sure that he would be glad to see me, I told Johnson to have his "shooting-irons"[1] ready and I would go up to them and see what they would do. As soon as they saw me coming they jumped up and drew their bows. I began to talk to them in their language. Yaiabi did not recognize me at first, and demanded to know what I was doing there. I told him I wanted water. He said there was no water except a very little they had brought with them. They asked me if I was alone. I told them that another young man was with me, then I called to Johnson to come up.

After Yaiabi found out who I was he felt better, for they were very uneasy at first. When I asked him how he came to be there, he said they had been out to a little lake to see some Parowan Indians that were camped there. I asked him what the Indians were doing there. He said they were waiting for some more of the Pocatello Indians to come, and as soon as they arrived they were going to burn all the stations and kill all of the riders and station keepers.

"Are you going with them?" I asked.

"No."

"Why then have you been with those Indians?"

He said that the Parowan Indians had stolen his sister's little boy two years before, and he went out to see if he could find the child.

"Did you find it?"

"No," he said, "they have sold it to the white folks."

[1] Revolvers or guns.

"Do you know when the Indians they are looking for will be there?"

"One sleep," [1] he said.

I knew it was a big day's ride back to where the Indians were gathering and I knew it was a hard day's ride to the place where the soldiers were camped. I did not know what was best for me to do. I had these two Indians and I did not want to let them go, for I was afraid they would skip back and let the others know that the soldiers were after them.

Here we were a big day's ride to water, and our horses had had none since early morning, so I decided that it would be better to take the Indians to headquarters and let General Johnston decide what to do. I told Yaiabi my plans. He said he did not want to go to the soldiers, for he was afraid of them. I told him I would see that the soldiers did him no harm. He said, "Yagaiki, you have known me ever since you were a little boy, and you never knew of my doing anything bad in your life." I told him I knew that he had always been a good Indian, "but now you know that the soldiers are after those bad Indians and intend to kill the last one of them, and if I let you go, you will go to them and tell them that the soldiers are after them. Then if General Johnston should find out what I had done he would think I stood in with the Indians and would have me shot; so, you see, you must go with us to the soldiers' camp."

The Indian that was with Yaiabi said he would not go to the soldiers' camp. He started to get his bow, but I had my pistol on him in a jiffy, and told him to stop. He stopped, and I kept him there while Johnson gathered up their bows and arrows. When I told them to get ready to start, Yaiabi said they were tired and would like to stay

[1] One night.

there until morning, but I said that our horses were so thirsty, we had better travel in the cool of the night or we should not be able to get them to camp, so we set out for Fish Springs.

I told Johnson to tie the bows and arrows to his saddle and to keep a close watch over them; Yaiabi mounted my horse while I walked and led the horse. When I got tired of walking, I changed places with Yaiabi, and then young Johnson walked and let the other Indian ride his horse. In this way we traveled until morning. When daylight came, I gave the bows and arrows to young Johnson and told him to go to General Johnston's camp as soon as possible and send us fresh horses and some water. In about six hours he came back to us, accompanied by two soldiers with some water and two extra horses for the Indians to ride. By traveling pretty fast, we reached camp at one o'clock that day.

General Johnston was very much pleased with me for bringing the two Indians in. At the sight of so many soldiers the Indians were very uneasy, but after they had been given something to eat and saw that they were not going to be hurt, they felt much better.

The General talked with the Indians for about an hour, and I acted as interpreter. Yaiabi told him just how the big camp of Indians was located, and said there were about three hundred warriors there then; they were looking for about fifty more to join them that night, and as soon as they could complete their plans they were going to burn the stations and kill all the white men they could find. He thought they would be ready in about five days to begin their bloody work.

The General liked the way Yaiabi talked. He called him a good Indian, and said he believed he was telling the truth. I told Yaiabi what the general said. General

Howard R. Driggs

Ruins of barracks at Camp Floyd, Utah; an army post established by Colonel Albert Sidney Johnston; also a home station for Pony Express and Overland Stage.

Johnston told me to get a little rest, for he wanted me to start out again that night if I would. I lay down and had a little sleep, and when I got up he told me that I was to go to the lake and see if Yaiabi had told the truth; and if everything was all right, to send back word as soon as I could by one of the scouts that he would send with me. He told me to do all my traveling at night and keep under cover in the daytime, and to meet him as soon as I could at a spring about half way between where we were and the Indians. Then on the following night he would move his soldiers to another spring which Yaiabi had told about, and which was within six miles of the lake where the Indians were gathering.

After dark, three of us started with four days' rations. I rode the little pinto pony on this trip, the first I had ridden him for a long time. We traveled all night and reached the first spring just at daybreak. I knew it would be a hard night's ride to go from here to the lake and then reach Yaiabi's spring in the mountains before daylight.

About midnight we arrived at the north end of the lake, which was only a mile and a half long and half a mile wide. I had my two scouts stop there while I wrapped a red blanket around me and went on foot to find out what I could about the Indian camp. I had gone only a few steps when I came to a band of horses, and as I was passing around them I heard an Indian speak to a horse he was hobbling. I went up and asked him in Shoshone if he had come with the Pocatello Indians. He said he had, and that seventeen others came with him.

"We will start burning the stations, then, soon," I said.

"Were you at the council tonight?" he asked. I told him I was not at the council, that I had been following a horse that had started back. He said that at the council it was decided that the Parowans were to go to Ruby Valley and burn and kill everything they came to; and that the Pocatello Indians and Gosiutes were to start at Ibapah and burn towards the east. I asked him when we were to start from there. He said, "In four days." We were walking towards their camp as we talked, so as soon as I found out all I wanted to know, I said that I had forgotten my rope and would have to go back for it. So I parted company with my Indian friend. He was a Shoshone, and he thought I was another. When I got out of his sight, I wasn't long getting back to where I had left the boys, and in a very short time one of them was carrying the news to the army.

The other scout and I went to find the spring Yaiabi had told me about. We got well into the mountains before daylight, and when it was light enough to see, we found the spring up a very rough canyon. We staked our horses so they could get plenty to eat and then crawled off into the willows for a good nap.

That afternoon I climbed a high mountain near by to see which would be the best way to go from there to the Indians' camp in the night. After I had studied the lay of the country pretty well, I went back to the horses, ate a little cold lunch, and when it commenced to get dark, we struck out to meet General Johnston at the appointed place.

We did not travel very fast, for I knew we would reach the place before the soldiers could get there. We were at the spring about two hours before daylight, and had a good nap before General Johnston came. When he got to us he wanted to know if I thought it safe to make a fire to boil some coffee. I told him I thought there was no danger, so we made a small fire, and had a good cup of coffee, then we all lay down for a little nap.

About sundown, the packers began loading the hundred pack mules we had with us, and we got started just about dark for the Yaiabi spring, which was about six miles north of the Indians' camp. We reached the spring in good time, and were all unpacked before dawn.

After breakfast, General Johnston and I went up on to the mountain so that he could see the Indian camp. He had a good pair of field glasses and could see everything very plainly. He asked if I knew anything about that bunch of willows he could see a little to the west of their camp. I told him I knew it very well, for when the express first started it came this way, and we had a station right where the Indian camp is now, so I had been there many times. He said, "Then you can take me to it in the night?" I told him I could, and pointed out to him the way we would have to go. He told me he wanted to make the attack the next morning at daybreak. We went back to camp, and found all the soldiers asleep, except the guard; and in a very short time we were rolled in our blankets and dreaming of the time when all the Indians would be good Indians.

When I awoke that afternoon, I saw General Johnston and his staff going up the mountain to where we had been that morning. They got back to camp just before sundown, and held a hasty council with the remainder of the officers; then orders were given to pack up, and we got in line just at dark. I told General Johnston he would have to take his men down this canyon in single file, and in some places we would have to travel along the side of the mountain over very narrow trails; that we would have to climb above high cliffs, and pass through some very dangerous places. He said that I was to go ahead, and, when I came to the bad places, to dismount and they would follow suit. We had about two miles to go before we would come to the bad places, and when I got off the next man would get off and so on down the line. By doing this, we got down the canyon very well, except that three of our pack mules rolled over a cliff and were killed.

The head of the company got out of the canyon about eleven o'clock that night. We were within six or seven hundred yards of the Indian camp, for the lake lay almost at the foot of the mountains. As the soldiers came down they formed into lines, and General Johnston and I started to find the bunch of willows we had seen from the top of the mountain. We soon found it, and went back to the soldiers. The general said that was all he wanted with me until after the fight, and told me to take care of the two Indians we had with us. So I got Yaiabi and his friend, and we climbed a small hill not far away, where we could see the fight when it commenced.

The soldiers didn't all get out of the canyon until about three o'clock in the morning, and the pack train was not all out when daylight came. In the meantime, General Johnston had strung the soldiers around the Indian camp.

Just as day was breaking, an old Indian chief started a fire in front of his tepee, and was standing there calling to some of the other Indians, when a soldier shot him without orders. Then the fight commenced. How the guns did rattle! It was almost too dark at first for me to see much of the fight, but it was getting lighter all the time. As we were coming down the canyon that night, the General gave me his field glasses to carry for him and I still had them.

Along the edge of the lake grew a lot of bulrushes. Soon after the firing began, I could see the papooses running into these rushes and hiding. From the volleys that were fired it got so smoky that I could not see very plainly, but the shooting soon stopped, and as the smoke rose, I could see everything that was going on. By this time they were in a terrible mixup, and were fighting fiercely, the soldiers with their bayonets and sabers, and the Indians with their clubs, axes, and knives. I could see little children not over five or six years old with sticks fighting like wildcats. I saw a soldier and an Indian that had clinched in a death struggle. They had each other by the hair of the head, and I saw a squaw run up to them with an ax and strike the soldier in the back and he sank to the ground, then she split his head with the ax. While she was doing this, a soldier ran a bayonet through her, and that is the way it was going over the whole battle ground. And what a noise they made! with the kids squalling, the squaws yelling, the bucks yelping, the dogs barking, and the officers giving their orders to the soldiers.

This was the worst battle and the last one that I ever saw. It lasted about two hours, and during that short period of time, every Indian, squaw, and papoose, and every dog was killed. After the battle, I was sent to bring up the baggage wagons to haul our wounded to Camp Floyd.

As we were on our way back to Camp Floyd with the wounded, and were passing through a rocky canyon, we were fired at by some straggling Indian, and I was shot through my left arm about half way between the wrist and elbow. The same bullet that went through my arm killed a soldier at my side. The one shot was all we heard, and we did not even see the one who fired it. I have sometimes wondered if that bullet was not sent especially for me.

That spring the great war between the North and the South broke out, and General Johnston sold all of the government cattle and wagons very cheap, and went back East with his pack mules. I bought a yoke of oxen for eighteen dollars and a new wagon for ten. There must have been as many as ten thousand oxen bought at from twenty-five to fifty dollars a yoke. That summer the gold mines were opened in Montana and everything had to be hauled with ox teams, and the same oxen we had bought for eighteen dollars were worth from one hundred and fifty to two hundred dollars a yoke. The poor people that had been living on greens and "lumpy dick" for two or three years now began to get very wealthy and proud. The young ladies began to wear calico dresses, and I even saw young men who could afford to wear calico shirts and soldiers' blue overcoats and smoke store tobacco.

20   THE OVERLAND STAGE

Just before the soldiers left Camp Floyd, the Overland Stage line was opened from St. Joseph, Missouri, to Sacramento, California. Shortly afterward the telegraph line was completed across the continent. This ended the work of the Pony Express. Instead of the pony riders dashing on their wiry horses over prairies and mountain and desert, now came the stage drivers with their sturdy horses, four or six-in-hand, rolling along in their great Concord coaches, loaded with passengers, mail, and express.

The stations, as before, were scattered along the trail from eight to sixteen miles apart, according to the water. These stations were mainly low dirt-roofed structures, built of logs or adobe or rock. After Johnston's army had decamped, the lumber left by them at Camp Floyd was used for some stations. They were large enough to accommodate six to eight horses, and had, partitioned from the stalls, one room for the stable keepers and another for provisions. Grain was hauled to them from the

168

fields of Utah and California. Native hay was supplied
from the grassy valleys through which the route lay.
Traveling blacksmiths kept the horses shod, and the
stages in repair.

As a few of the stations had to be built where there was
no spring or stream, it was necessary to haul water to
them. This was my first work in connection with the
Overland Stage. I had a good four-horse team and was
given the job of supplying Canyon station with water.

One day while I was unloading the water the stage came
into this station. Major Howard Egan, who had charge
of this division of the route, had the lines. The stage
driver lay dead in "the boot" and one passenger was
wounded. They had been shot by stage robbers, or
"road agents," as we called them. Another driver must
be had. The station keepers said they couldn't drive
four horses, so Major Egan called on me. I hadn't had
any experience handling the stage, but I tried it. The
Major seemed to think I drove all right, for he didn't
send any man to relieve me as he promised to do, so I
kept on driving. Finally I sold my team and water out-

An overland stage ready for a trip.

fit and became a regular stage driver. For about two years I kept on swinging over the rough and heavy roads through the deserts of Nevada in the "boot" of the Concord stage.

The "boot" was the place where the driver sat perched in front. It was big enough to hold two passengers besides the driver; and a thousand pounds or more of mail could be packed in the "boot" also. Behind this was the body of the coach, big enough to hold six passengers. They sat three on each seat, facing each other. It was hard on those not used to it to sit day and night through clouds of alkali dust or sand, through rain and slush, or snow and cold, cramped up in that stage. If we had to crowd more than six in, as we did occasionally, it was rather rough riding. When few passengers were along, or the mail was lighter, we made up our load with grain or other provisions to be distributed along at the various stations. So we were nearly always well loaded. Often we carried more than a ton of mail in the "boot," and strapped on the back platform.

Some pictures I have seen of the Overland Stage have passengers on top. This is a mistake. There was no place on the rounded top for passengers. Some of the boys occasionally lashed packages there. The passengers would have had to be strapped on too, if they had tried the top, for they would have got pitched off in a hurry, the stage rocked so. The body of the stage was hung on great leather springs, and it swung with a kind of cradle motion as we dashed along. When a fellow learned how to swing with it, things went all right; if he didn't, it was hard riding.

The road was not only rough and wearisome; it was dangerous. For a time the Indians were so troublesome that a soldier was sent with every stage. We should have

Two Gosiute braves of Overland Stage days.

felt safer without these soldiers though, for we knew how the Indians hated soldiers. The worst danger, however, was not from Indians; they got lots of blame that didn't belong to them. It was the "road agents" that infested the country during those days that gave us most trouble.

Many a time these desperadoes would hold up the stage on some lonely place on the road. They would spring out before the horses and order the driver to stop, or would shoot down a horse to stop the stage; then after robbing the passengers and rifling the mail bags of their valuables, they would dash away with their plunder to their hiding places in the hills.

Some drivers, when these outlaws came upon them, would put the whip to their horses and try to dash by them to safety. At times the boys managed to give the robbers the slip, but oftener the driver would be shot down in the attempt to escape. Then the horses, mad with fright, if no passenger was aboard to grab the lines, would run away, upset the coach, perhaps, and string things along the trail in great shape. Sometimes they have dashed into a station with nothing but the front wheels dragging behind them.

I was lucky enough to escape such mishaps. The robbers never held me up; but one day I did have one of my wheel horses shot down, by some skulking desperado or

Indian, we never knew which. I was swinging along a dugway down hill about two miles west of Canyon station when it happened. Three passengers — two men and a woman — were in the stage. A shot rang out and my off wheel horse dropped dead.

I flung off the brake, knowing what was up, cracked my whip and away we went plunging down the hill, dragging the dead horse with us till I thought we were out of gunshot. No more shots came, so I stopped the team, jumped down and began to unhitch. The man inside the coach jumped out too, but instead of helping me, he grabbed the whip and begun to lash the team, yelling to me to go on. He was so scared he acted like a crazy man till his wife jumped out, grabbed the whip from his hand, and told him to behave himself. Then he cooled down a little; and with the help of the other passenger, I got the dead horse out of the harness, hitched one of the leaders in his place, and drove on to the next station, without any more trouble. I never found out who did that devilish trick, but I don't believe it was stage robbers, though, for they would have followed us up and finished their mischief. Other drivers, however, were not so lucky. Three different times Major Egan brought in the

Antelope Jake, an aged Gosiute Indian who won his name by killing antelope for Overland Stage stations.

stage with the driver dead in the boot and the stage shot full of holes. At one time a driver who had been wounded by outlaws was loaded into my stage. We were trying to get him through to Salt Lake, but the poor fellow died while he was with me. No other passenger was along at the time. I couldn't help the sufferer much. It was a terrible experience, I tell you, for him and me too, that long night on the lonely Nevada desert.

Afterwards I was changed to another division, driving in Nevada from Austin to Sand Wells. Jim Clift was division agent here. It was a heavy road, — full of sand; but it wasn't so hard and heavy as another stretch that Ben Halliday, our big chief, gave me later. When he heard I was careful with the horses, that I didn't use them up as did some of the drivers they brought in from the East, who didn't know mountain life, he set me to driving from the Sink of Carson to Fort Churchill. I drove there that summer and winter and the next spring

Antelope on the desert. Pictures of this kind were often seen by Pony Express riders.

Old stage station at Fort Hall or Ross's Fork, Idaho.

I was sent to drive from Carson City to Virginia City, Nevada.

I arrived at Carson City about ten o'clock one very fine morning in June. The mail agent met me just as I entered the town, and told me to drive to Tim Smith's big rock stable and put up my horses. He told me that the line I was driving on was in dispute, and he would have to go to Salt Lake City to see who had the right of way. "Stay here until you hear from me," he said, "and board in that hotel across the street." With that he left me alone, seven hundred miles from home and among strangers. If he had left me in an Indian camp, I should have felt all right; but to be left away out here among a lot of strange white folks was more than I could bear.

I put my horses up, and while I was sitting out by the side of the stable, I saw a man come out of the hotel. He had on a white cap, and a white apron that reached from his chin to his feet. In each hand he had a big, round, brass thing. He pounded these together and made a fearful racket. I had never seen a hotel before, to say nothing of being in one, and as the men that worked in the barn came rushing past me, I asked one of them what was up. "Dinner," he said. I got up and went over to the hotel, and when I went in, I never saw such a sight before. They had tables all over the house, and people were rushing in and sitting down to them.

I slipped in and took off my hat and stood by the side of the door waiting for some one to come up and ask me to sit down at a table, but nobody came. I stood there a while longer, and saw others come in and sit down at the tables without being asked, so I went sneaking up to a table and stood there, and as nobody asked me to sit down, I sat down anyhow. A waiter came up and began to mutter something to me. I asked, "What?" He got it off again. I told him that I did not know what he said, so he went out and brought me something to eat. I went over to the stable and sat down, and then I began thinking of home. I didn't go back to the hotel that night for any supper, and when I went to bed, the fleas were so bad I didn't sleep a wink that night, and when morning came I was hungry, sleepy, tired, and homesick.

Next morning I met one of the stable men. He asked me if I had been to breakfast. I told him I had not. "Come right on in," he said, taking me by the arm. The waiter came up and got off the same thing that he said the day before, and the man that was with me told him to fetch it along. I told the waiter to bring me the same. Well, I ate two or three breakfasts that morning to make up. Then I felt much better.

After breakfast we went back to the stable, and pretty soon Tim Smith came in and said, "Young man, it may be three weeks before the right of way is settled, but if you want to go to work in the stable I will give you three dollars a day." I agreed and began to work. Tim Smith was a one-armed man, and he had fourteen hostlers and a clerk that worked in the stable. The office was in one corner of the stable and a young man by the name of Billy Green was the clerk. He had charge of the men and was very kind and good to me.

I was afraid to go out at night, so I stayed in the stable and helped Billy. It was a very large stable, holding over one hundred horses, and there was a good deal of work to do after dark.

At that time Virginia City was booming. Two or three men were killed every day. I had not driven here very long before I saw a man hanged at what they called the Golden Gate. I don't remember what he had done, but I saw him hanged, anyway.

Those were rough, wild days, and this was one of the roughest spots in the savage West. I was glad enough to leave it. After a few months of staging here, I quit the job and returned home.

Spring at Rockwell's stage station, Salt Lake County, Utah.

" All of us but the driver would walk ahead of the team."

21   A TERRIBLE JOURNEY

WHEN I returned from Nevada to Utah, I found that
mother had moved to Cache Valley, so I went up there
and stayed all winter with her. It proved to be a very
sad winter for me, though it began very happily. I found
here my first sweetheart, a beautiful girl, who made me
love her very dearly by her sweet ways and her kind
heart; for she helped my mother nurse me through a
dangerous illness.

We had spent the time delightfully for about a month,
when I got hurt. My horse, which I was riding one day
very fast, struck some ice, slipped and fell, throwing me
to the ground. My head struck the ice so hard that it
nearly killed me. I was carried home; brain fever came
on and I lay in bed till spring. To make matters worse,
the wound in my head broke out again and I was delirious
for part of the time. But this dear girl stayed by my
bedside day after day, and helped me past death's door.
They thought I was dying one day, and she was driven

half wild for fear I might go ; but the next day I had rallied and from then on I recovered very fast.

Our intention was to get married ; but before we coul l realize our hopes they were blighted and destroyed by certain men who should have been our friends. These men poisoned the minds of her parents against me, while I was away driving the stage and guarding the cattle of the people against the Indians ; her parents refused to allow her to answer my letters ; and finally they succeeded in making her give me up and marry one of the men who had turned them against me.

The little bunch of cattle, which I had bought with the money I had received for my team, were stolen that winter, presumably by the Indians. I hunted for them for a while, but not one did I ever get back. The money I had saved for a "wedding stake," I gave to mother ; and as I had no heart to stay in that town any longer, I started for the road again.

That summer I worked for John Bolwinkle of Salt Lake City, as his wagon boss, in charge of his ox-team freighting from Carson City, Nevada. A mail route had been established from Salt Lake City to Bannock, Montana, and Mr. Leonard I. Smith obtained the contract to carry this mail. Knowing of my experience in this business, he induced me to drive the stage from Salt Lake north that winter.

We started out some time in November with a wagonload of dry goods to trade for horses along the road. Besides this, we had one light coach and two buggies, in which were seven passengers. We went on our journey through Ogden, Brigham City, and other towns north, buying what horses we could as we went along. For a few days we stopped at Soda Springs to arrange about making a mail station there. At that time a large company of soldiers were wintering in the town. It was the plan of Mr. Smith to make me division agent from Soda Springs to Salt Lake, but I was to go on with him to Bannock to get acquainted with the whole route.

When we got to Bannock, winter had set in. It snowed very hard while we were there, and kept snowing all of the way back. By the time we got to Snake River, the snow was deep, and there was no place where we could buy feed for our horses. We had two passengers with us, and Mr. Smith had not provided us with supplies enough to last us half way back to Soda Springs.

We could not travel as fast as he had planned on account of the deep snow, and the horses were getting very weak for want of food. For these reasons we could not come back on the road by which we had gone, so we kept down the Snake River to where the Blackfoot empties into it. There we ate the last of our provisions. We were still one hundred miles from any place where we could get more, and the snow was becoming deeper every day. When we got up the Ross Fork Canyon we had to stop for the night. Here three of the horses gave out, and we had to leave them and one of the buggies. We had left the coach at Beaver Canyon.

The next morning we started before breakfast, for we had eaten the last thing the morning before. The snow kept falling all the time, and by noon, it was at least three feet deep. All of us but the driver would walk ahead of the team to break the road. We had four horses on the buggy, and the buggy would push up the snow ahead of it until it would run in over the dashboard and sides. That day two more of the horses gave out and we had to leave them, but we reached the head of the Portneuf.

That night we all turned out and kicked the snow off a little space so the poor horses could get some frozen grass, but it was so very cold and they were so tired that they could not eat very much.

The next morning we made another early start, and Mr. Smith said we would get to Soda Springs that day, but I knew we could not get there that day, nor the next day, either. I told the passengers that if we were to leave the buggy, we might make it in two days, but the way we were fooling along with the worn-out horses, we never would get there. They told Mr. Smith what I said and he upbraided me for it. He said I had scared the passengers nearly to death and he wanted me to stop.

Well, by noon that day, we came to the road we had come out on, but Mr. Smith did not know the place and wanted to follow the road over which we had traveled in going to Bannock. I told him the way we wanted to go was south, but the way he wanted to go was north. He told me I was wrong and ordered me to keep still. "Well," I said, "I will go to Soda Springs and you can go to the other place," so I took what I wanted out of the buggy and started off, but I had not gone far when I heard some one calling me. It was so foggy and the frost was falling so fast that I could see only a few yards, and as I hesitated about going back, one of the passengers came up to me and asked me if I was sure I knew where I was going, and begged me to come back to the buggy.

One of the passengers was a large, strong Irishman, and appeared to be well educated; the other was a sickly looking Englishman. I don't remember their names, but they called each other Mike and Jimmy. I went back to the buggy and Mike saw that I did not want anything to say to Mr. Smith, so he did the talking. He questioned Mr. Smith and then me for quite a while, and then he said he believed that I was right. He told the driver to

Caspar W. Hodgson

A snowy road through an Idaho forest.

turn the team around and follow me. The driver obeyed although it made Mr. Smith very angry.

After turning south we had not traveled over four miles, when one of the remaining horses gave out and we could not get the poor thing to move, so we had to leave the buggy. We went on about three or four hundred yards to a clump of quaking aspen, and built a large fire. When we all got warm, I went to bring up the horses and buggy, and when I got back to the fire, Mr. Smith and Mike were quarreling. Mr. Smith said that we were going away from Soda Springs, and that he intended to turn and go the other way.

It was already quite dark, but we could travel just as well in the night as in the day, for we could not see very far anyhow on account of the fog. I said I knew I was right and for all those who wanted to go to Soda Springs to fall in line, for I was going to start right then. I went to the buggy and got a pair of buffalo moccasins I had there, put them on, and started down the trail. "Hold on," called Mike, "I will go with you." Then Jimmy said he was not going to stay there and starve to death, that he would go with us, too. So the three of us went our way and left Mr. Smith and the driver standing there in the fog and snow.

It was about eleven o'clock at night when we left the buggy. We did not feel much like pushing our way through the snow, for we had already walked many miles that day, and had been three days without anything to eat. Mike said he would take the lead to break the path, I was to come next, and Jimmy was to follow me. There was about a foot of snow with a crust on it, not quite hard enough to hold one up, and on top of this was about two feet of lighter snow, so you see it was very hard traveling.

We had not been out over two hours, when Mike said

his feet were frozen. I had a few matches in my pocket wrapped in paper, and we kicked around to find some dry sagebrush, but it was all wet and frozen. We broke up some and tried to make a fire, but it would not burn. Pretty soon Mike said we should give him the matches and he would try it. He took them and laid them down by his side while trying to light one, and Jimmy came up, struck them with his foot, and scattered them all through the snow. We could not find a single one of them, so we had to go without any fire.

We trudged along, stumbling over sagebrush and rock until morning. Mike said we must be very near Soda Springs, for he thought we had traveled twenty miles or more during the night, and he could not believe me when I told him we had not made over eight miles. I told them before we left the buggy that it was about thirty miles to Soda Springs, so I knew we had over twenty miles yet.

Jimmy and I were about played out, and had to stop every little while to rest. Mike had long legs, but Jimmy and I were so short that when we tried to step in his tracks we had to jump, and that made it harder for Jimmy and me. During the night we had traveled too far to the east and had left the trail through the lava beds and sagebrush, and had started to cross the big meadow and swamps along the Blackfoot River. The tall slough grass and bulrushes were so tangled and frozen together that we could hardly get through them. Sometimes Mike would forget himself and step about six feet over a large mass of grass and rushes, and Jimmy and I would have to wallow through them.

About noon the fog rose a little and we could see a large butte which we called the Chinaman's Hat, and which I knew was twelve miles from Soda Springs. The butte was about four miles ahead of us, which would make it sixteen miles from where we were to Soda. Jimmy said his feet were frozen, and that he was too tired to go much farther. I was about worn out, too, so we were in a pretty bad fix. The fog soon settled again, and was so thick that we could not see fifty yards, and we were all so tired out that I knew we could not reach the Chinaman's Hat before ten o'clock that night.

We decided that we must not stop to rest more than ten minutes at any time, and that at least one of us must keep awake, for we knew that if all went to sleep at the same time we would never again wake up.

It was a bitter cold night. There was no wind blowing, and it was very still, not even a bird, rabbit, or coyote was to be seen or heard — not a sound but the ringing in our ears. By this time I had gotten over my being hungry, but I was very thirsty, and I had eaten so much snow to satisfy my thirst that my mouth and tongue had become so sore and swollen that I could scarcely speak. Jimmy was so used up by this time that we could hardly get him to move after we had stopped to rest, and Mike would sometimes carry him a little way; but Jimmy said it hurt him, so Mike would have to put him down again.

Well, night was coming on again, and I do not think we had traveled over three or four miles that day, but we were doing the best we could. About four o'clock in the afternoon we stopped for a minute's rest; I settled back in the snow and put one foot out for Jimmy to lay his head on. Soon it was time to start again and I shook Jimmy, but he did not stir. Mike had already started, so I pulled my foot out from under Jimmy's head, and as I did so his head sank in the snow. Then I took hold of him and tried to raise him, but I could not. I called for Mike, and when he came back, we raised Jimmy up, and I saw that he was dead.

I cannot tell you what happened in the next half hour, but from what he said in his sorrow over Jimmy's death, I learned for the first time that Jimmy had married Mike's sister. After a while I scraped the snow away clear to the ground, and while doing this, I found a dry thistle stalk about fourteen inches long. I took the dead man's coat off, laid him in the hole, spread the coat over his face, and covered him with snow, making a little mound like a grave. I tore some of the lining from my coat, tied it to the thistle, and stuck it over the grave.

It was hard work to get Mike started again. He said we were all going to die anyway, and he would rather stay there with Jimmy. I told him we were nearly to Soda Springs, and if he would try, we could get there; but he said I had told him that so much that he didn't believe I knew where Soda Springs was. He said I had

Shoshone tepee. Brush across entrance
means " No one at home."

told him when we first started from the buggy that it was only thirty miles and he knew we had traveled over seventy miles by this time. I told him I knew if we traveled as fast as we could that we would be in Soda Springs in two hours.

We talked there a long time, and I began to think that Mike had really made up his mind not to try to go on any more, when just before dark he seemed to take fresh courage. He jumped up and started out so fast that I could not keep up with him. After a while he stopped and sat down again in the snow, and when I caught up to him I found him sound asleep. I let the poor fellow sleep a few minutes, and then I found it almost impossible to wake him. After pulling and shaking him, I finally got him on his feet, but he would start off the wrong way. Then I would get hold of him and start him off right, but he would turn around and go the wrong way. He did not know what he was doing, so I had to take the lead. Then he would stop and I would have to go back and get him.

After a little time he seemed to come to himself, and took the lead again for about a mile, and then he sat down in the snow and said he was done for, and that he would not go another step. I did all I could to rouse him, but he would not stir. He gave me a small memorandum book and a little buckskin bag full of gold dust, and told me he had a sister living in Mississippi, and that I would find her address in the book. I talked to him a long time to try to get him to come with me, but he would not move.

I saw that it was of no use, and that I would have to leave him or lie down in the snow and die with him. This I felt like doing, but for the sake of my mother and sisters, I thought I would make one more effort to reach the

town, so I left him and had gone about seventy-five
yards, when I stumbled over something and fell head-
long into the snow. I cleared the snow away from my
face, and sat there thinking about home and how badly
my mother would feel if she knew where I was, and how
easy it would be to lie there in the snow and go to sleep.

Drowsiness had nearly overcome me when, suddenly, I
heard the far-away tinkle of a bell. I knew then that I was
not far from Soda Springs. I jumped up and ran back to
Mike as fast as I could go, and when I got to him, I found
him stretched out on the snow with his hands folded
over his breast and sound asleep. It was all but impossible
to wake him. I am certain he would have died if he had
been left ten minutes longer. When I got him awake
enough to tell him about the bell, the sound had ceased.
He would not believe what I told him about it, so I could
not get him to come with me.

I went back to the place where I first heard the bell and
sat down again. In a few minutes I heard it louder than
before. Then I rushed back to Mike and found him
awake, and when I got him to listen he heard the bell this
time, too. He jumped up and started so fast in the direction of the sound that I could not keep up with him.
When he would see me falling behind, he would come back
and take hold of my hands and pull me along. I begged
him to let me alone and told him it hurt me to be jerked
over the snow in that way. Then he would kick the
snow and say that he would make a good road for me if I
would only come.

We had traveled this way for about half an hour, when
the fog rose a little and we saw, a short distance ahead
of us, a faint light. He then left me and started for
the light as fast as he could go. I tried to follow, but
slipped and fell, and found that I could not get up again.

Many times I tried to rise, but fell back every time. I thought if I lay there a while and rested, then perhaps I could get up and go on. I guess I must have fallen asleep, for the first thing I knew, two men had hold of me and were carrying me to the hotel where we had seen the light. Mike had reached there and had told the men in the hotel that one of his companions was dead and another was out there just a little way dying in the snow.

When we got to the door, Mike was standing there with a big glass of whiskey in his hand. "Down this, old boy," he said, "and it will be the making of you," but I could not bear the smell of this liquor, to say nothing of drinking it.

They set me down in a chair near the stove, but the heat soon made me feel sick, and I had to move as far from the fire as I could get. The cook brought something for us to eat, but my mouth and tongue hurt me so that I could hardly eat anything. Then the light began to grow dim and I could feel them shaking me and could hear them talking to me, but I could not answer, for my tongue was so swollen. Then I seemed to go away off.

The next thing I remember, they were telling me that the doctors had come, and I saw that the house was full of people. They told me that Mike's feet were frozen and that two men were holding them in a tub of cold water to try to draw the frost out. The doctor was pulling my moccasins off and I heard him say that my feet were all right. It seems that they were giving me hot soup or something every minute, but I was so sleepy that I hardly knew what was going on. I soon found myself in bed with two doctors standing over me. One of them was the faithful Doctor Palmer who, years afterwards, became a dear friend and neighbor of mine. He told me they had just brought in the dead man, and that they did not know what to do with him until either Mike or I was able to talk. They were going to hold an inquest over the body and wanted witnesses to tell how he died. I tried to ask if they had sent for Mr. Smith, but they could not understand what I said.

I don't know how much time had passed, when an army officer came in and began talking to Doctor Palmer. I heard Doctor Palmer say, "Is that so?" The officer said it was. Then Doctor Palmer said, "I did not know he was that bad." I rose to ask what was the matter, but Doctor Palmer told me to lie still. The officer said, "Shall I tell him?" Doctor Palmer said, "Not now, let the other doctor tell him." The officer went out and soon the old doctor came in. He told me that the man who came with me had his feet so badly frozen that he could not save them and they would have to be taken off. He said he would leave Sergeant Chauncey with me while Doctor Palmer assisted him in cutting off Mike's feet. He told me to keep very quiet and in a few days I would be all right.

About two hours after Mike and I reached the hotel, a company of men started out to find Mr. Smith; and when they reached the buggy, they found Mr. Smith and the driver all right. They had the meat of two horses cut up and hanging in the trees. When they told Mr. Smith that Mike and I had reached Soda Springs but that Jimmy was dead, he said he was surprised that we were not all dead, for he was certain that I was leading them right away from the town.

The party that went out for Mr. Smith got back the day the doctors were going to cut Mike's feet off. Mr. Smith came in to see me, and he almost cried when he saw the fix I was in. He said he would take me right to Salt Lake City, where I would get better care than I could in

S. N. Leek, Jackson, Wyoming

Wnter scene near Uncle Nick's home in Jackson's Hole. Thousands of elk come into this valley during the " snowy moons."

Soda Springs. They would not allow him to move me, however, though he tried his hardest to take me.

Owing to the skill of Doctor Palmer I got along pretty well, but it was several weeks before I was able to get around very much. Poor Mike suffered terribly after his feet were taken off, but he got well and strong as ever, except for the loss of his feet.

When I got well, I drove the mail from Soda Springs to Franklin during the rest of the winter. That June Jimmy's wife came out from Mississippi. She was Mike's sister, and a most beautiful woman.

She and Mike induced me to stop driving the mail for a while and take them back over the road we traveled those awful days to reach Soda Springs. I secured a buggy for us to ride in, a small spring wagon to carry the camp outfit, and a good cook to go with us to do the cooking and drive the mess wagon.

We first stopped where Jimmy died. The spot was still marked by the pieces of my coat lining that were lying around. Then we went to where we had left Mr. Smith and his driver. When we reached the place where Mr. Smith wanted to turn north and follow the old trail in the wrong direction, Mike told his sister that if it had not been for me that day, they would all have gone the wrong way and there, somewhere on that lonely trail, have perished in the snow. From there we went to the Snake River, where we had eaten our last meal on that awful trip.

We found here a large band of Indians, and among them were several that I was acquainted with. We could not get away from them, they were so glad to see me, so we stayed here four days. They wanted to know why I didn't come back in those days and live with them all the time. Then I had to tell them all about where I had been ever since I went away from them and what I had been doing all that time. They took turns asking me questions until I thought they would talk me to death.

These were the first Indians this woman had ever seen, and she was frightened of them until she noticed how glad they were to see me and how kind they were; then she felt better towards them. She said she was delighted to hear me talk to them, that they were certainly a queer people, and that I must have been a strange boy to leave my home and go to live with them.

After I had finished my visit with the Indians we turned back over the same road. When we got to mother's home, Mike and his sister stayed with us three weeks. They kept trying all the time to induce me to go with them to her home in Mississippi, but my mother objected so strongly that I would not go, although I wanted to very much. They would have treated me very kindly, I am sure. They even offered to share their property with me; but I thought more of my mother than I did of anybody else in the world and I could not leave her to make my home among strangers.

22   MY OLD SHOSHONE FRIENDS

"WHAT became of your old Indian mother, Washakie,
Hanabi, and the rest?" This question has been asked
me again and again. "Did you ever see them again?"
"What other experiences did you have with the Indians?"
Such queries as these have been sent to me from even
far-off France by people who have read the first edition
of my little book.

To satisfy my readers on these points and others that
may be of interest, I have added a few more chapters to
my story.

When I left my dear old Indian mother up north on
"Pohogoy," or Ross Fork, — a place near the Snake River,
— I promised her I would come back to her. That promise
I intended to keep; but I was prevented from doing so
by other pressing duties, till it was too late.

She waited a year for her "Yagaki" to return, then her
sorrow became so great she couldn't bear it longer and
she started out to hunt me up. The Indians told me
later that after I had been gone a few months my old

mother would roam off in the mountains and lonely places and stay until hunger would drive her home. Finally she came to my white mother's home in Grantsville to find her boy. My mother made her welcome, taking my Indian mother into her home, feeding her, and providing her with a room as one of the family.

Then she wrote me that my two mothers wanted me to come home. I wished with all my heart to do so, but at that time I was about five hundred miles away, out on the mail line, badly wounded in the head by an Indian arrow. When I recovered enough to travel, I had to go to work again. The Indians at this time were burning stations and killing men every chance they got. Riders became so scarce and hard to get that I could not well leave, no matter how I felt.

When I finally did get away, I found that my own mother, as I have said before, had moved into Cache Valley, and my old Indian mother had left her, broken-hearted because she had not found her papoose. She had stayed with my white mother for more than two months. When I did not return as she expected, she grew suspicious that my white mother had hidden me away; and no words could comfort her or change her mind. Finally she went off with some Indians who came there.

My mother urged me to hunt her up. She had taken quite a fancy to the Indian woman. She thought it my duty to find and care for her the rest of her life. I felt so too. She had been a dear friend to me. She had cared for me and protected me from harm, even saving my life several times.

The next word I got of my Indian mother was that she was dead. This sad news came from a band of Shoshones I found in the Bear Lake Valley. Hearing they were

Bureau of American Ethnology, Smithsonian Institution

Washakie's encampment at South Pass, Wyoming, 1861. South Pass is a pass through the Rocky Mountains, where the Oregon and Salt Lake trails crossed the Continental Divide.

there, I had gone to see them, thinking to meet some of my old Indian friends. But those I wished most to see were not among the band. My dear old mother, they told me, had died about three years after I left. Washakie was then out in the Wind River country. As these Indians were going there, I decided to go with them.

We found Washakie at South Pass. He was very glad to see me, and treated me like a brother. But he could not tell me just where our mother was buried, as he had happened to be away from her when she died. He only knew that her grave was somewhere on Ham's Fork [1] in Wyoming. He found an Indian who said he knew where it was. I offered to give him a pony if he would guide me to it. He agreed, and we went back to the head of Ham's Fork. We found the camping place they were at when she died, but not the grave, though we hunted for three days together, and I stayed another day after he left. Since then I have passed the place many times and have searched again and again; for I did desire to carry out my old Indian mother's wish to be buried like the whites, but I have never found her grave.

It was the custom of the Indians to bury their dead in some cleft of rocks or wash. They left no mark over the grave, but they usually buried with the body articles the deceased had treasured in life, as weapons, clothing, etc. In the grave with my dear old mother they placed the beaded and tasseled quiver she had made of the skin of the antelope I had killed, the auger I had sent to Salt Lake for, and other things of mine she had kept after I went away. There are those who think an Indian has no heart. This dear old woman certainly had one that was tender and true. Her soul was good and pure. Peace to her memory.

[1] A branch of the Green River.

Washakie's wife Hanabi was another good woman. She, too, had died before I returned to the Indians. Her little girl papoose, the baby when I was with them, grew up, I have been told, and married.

Washakie married another squaw by whom he had several children. One of them, Dick Washakie, is still living in the Wind River country. He is a wealthy Indian, and has considerable influence.

When these Shoshone Indians made their treaty with the government there were three reservations set apart for the Shoshone tribe — Fort Hall, Lemhi, and Wind River. Washakie was given his choice. He took the Wind River reserve because, as he told me afterwards, it had been his boyhood home, and his father was buried there. Here Washakie spent the rest of his life, honored by his tribe and respected for his goodness and his wisdom by all the whites who knew him. During the early nineties he passed to the Happy Hunting Grounds.

I saw Washakie many times before he died. We were always brothers. When I lived in Bloomington, Bear Lake County, Idaho, the chief often came and stayed with me. He was always made welcome in my home, and his lodge was always open to me. During the time of Chief Joseph's War, Washakie brought his band and camped for some months near my ranch on Bear River; and every day he would come to get the news of the war. My wife would read the paper and I would interpret it for the Indians.

While this war was on, the whites would not sell ammunition to the Indians without a letter of recommendation, or "Tabop," as they called it. The Indians all came to me for these letters. My home for years was their headquarters. They would have eaten me out of house and home if the ward authorities had not come to my rescue and helped to feed these Red Brethren.

23   TRAPPING WITH AN INDIAN

BUT the Indians were not always a burden. They
sometimes gave me good help. At one time in particular
I found an Indian who proved a friend in need. It was
during the winter of 1866-7, the year after I had brought
my wife from Oxford, Idaho, to Bloomington.

"Hogitsi," a Shoshone Indian, with his family, was
wintering in the town at the time. The whites called
him "Hog," but he hadn't a bit of the hog in his nature.
I found him to be one of the best Indians I ever knew.

After I had got well acquainted with him, he proposed
that we try trapping to make some money. I was hard
up; my family was destitute of food and clothing, for I
had hard luck that summer, so I was ready to try anything.

We set to work over in Nounan Valley on a little stream
about fifteen miles from home. The results were very
encouraging. At the end of the first week we came back
with sixty dollars' worth of furs. It was the easiest
money I ever made in my life. Such success made us
ready to try again.

A mink.

New York Zoölogical Society

"Hog" proposed that we go down to the Portneuf country and spend the winter at the trapping business. He said he knew of a stream there that was full of beaver and mink and other fur animals. I was anxious to go, but my wife protested that she could not think of my going off for a whole winter with an Indian. She was sure I would be scalped. It was hard work for me to persuade her that under our circumstances it was the right thing to do. She finally consented, however, and we set to work to get ready.

With "Hog" to help we soon had enough winter's wood chopped up to last my family through the winter. I did all I could otherwise to leave them comfortable; but the best I could do was not enough to keep them from having a hard time of it while I was away.

I had three horses. "Hog" got two more from Thomas Rich; and Joseph Rich, who kept a store in Paris, supplied us with provisions and camp outfit upon our agreeing to sell to him what furs we should get.

It was about a week after New Year's that we struck out northward through the cold and snow. The snow got deeper and deeper as we went on towards Soda Springs.

It seemed impossible to make our destination. I suggested that we turn back, but "Hog" wouldn't listen to me. He said that we would find the snow lighter from there on, and it would be only a day or two more before we got to the Portneuf. So I yielded and we pushed on till we reached Dempsey Creek, a branch of the Portneuf. Here we made our winter camp at the base of the lava cliffs that border the stream near where it empties into the Portneuf. We chose a good place on the sunny side of the rock, and built our quarters. A cleft up the face of the cliff served us well. By building up a fourth side to this cleft, we made a fine chimney and fireplace. Around this we made our shack — of quaking aspen poles and willows, and long grass to thatch it. For a door we used the skins of two white-tailed deer stretched over a quaking aspen frame. Our house was a cosy shelter from the storms, and roomy enough to store

New York Zoölogical Society

Beaver and beaver lodge.

our bales of furs. For wood we used cedar, which grew near by.

Within the cedars we found plenty of black-tail deer, while in the willows the white-tail were so numerous that we had little trouble to get all we needed. Trout we could catch at any time; so we had food in abundance.

When it came to trapping, we found beaver and mink so thick that it was no trick at all to catch them. Otter were not so plentiful, but we did land several of these beautiful animals.

I tended the traps and did the cooking. Hogitsi skinned the animals, stretched the fur, and kept watch of the horses. He was a good worker — not a lazy thing about him. Usually he was in bed an hour before me, and up an hour earlier. By the time I was ready to tumble out, he had the fire roaring, and was at work on the skins. While I got breakfast, he would look after the horses, and bring my old buckskin mare to camp. After breakfast I would get on her and ride the rounds of the traps to see what luck the night had brought. Usually I found the traps all sprung and a beaver or mink or sometimes an otter in them, tail up, and drowned in the stream. For we weighted the traps with a rock to hold the animal, when caught, under water. If the animal is not drowned, he will often gnaw off his foot and get away. After taking out the game, I would reset the traps, and return to camp with my load.

To keep the traps going kept me busy all day. We caught animals so fast that I had sometimes to stop and help Hogitsi catch up with his skinning and stretching. We would sit up at times late at night at this work. Evidently little trapping, if any, had ever been done on this stream, for the animals seemed not to know what a trap meant.

If it hadn't been for the worry I had for my dear ones at home, the winter would have been a pleasant one in every way. It was one of the easiest I ever spent, and most profitable. I never have made money faster than I did that winter. When springtime came, we had about seven hundred pounds of fur. At that time mink and beaver skins sold at two dollars per pound; otter was worth one dollar a foot. A stretched otter skin would often bring nine dollars or more.

When we turned over our pack to Mr. Rich, we found we had $900.00 due us after paying all our expenses. He paid us in gold, silver, and greenbacks. Hogitsi was scared when he saw the pile; and when it came to dividing, he certainly proved that he was no hog; for he simply would not take his full share. He insisted that we should not have had any if it hadn't been for me; that it would "make him too rich."

This streak of good luck gave me a new start. My wife felt better about the trapping business; but she had no desire to repeat the experience of that winter; and, as I found other profitable work to do, I did not turn to trapping again as a business, though I have done a good deal of this work at various times since. And I have also done a good deal of trading in furs with the trappers.

This trading has brought me into acquaintanceship with a good many of the mountaineers. It was through this that I came to know Kit Carson, who came to my home hunting his trapper son-in-law, Sims, one winter. Sims was wintering near at the time. Kit stopped over night with me. I brought his son-in-law to my home and they made up their troubles. Kit wanted to stay with me for a while. I took him in, and we boarded and lodged him for several months. We had a good time together swapping yarns that winter, I can tell you.

24   WORKING ON THE INDIAN RESERVATION

WHEN the government undertook the task of settling the Indians on the reservations, I was given the job of helping the Indian Agent of the Fort Hall reservation gather and keep the Redmen within bounds. This was no easy task. The Indians found it hard, after their many years of roving life, to be restrained. They often grew discontented, complaining at times that they were being cheated and otherwise mistreated. It is a well-known fact that they often had much cause to complain. The Indians have been abused shamefully by the whites at times, and I know it. Our dealings with the Redmen reflect no great credit on us.

If the Indians became disgruntled, as they frequently did, they would slip away to the mountains in a sulky mood. Whenever they did this, it was my business to bring them back. This task was not only disagreeable, but sometimes dangerous.

At one time a band under the lead of old Sagwich got angry over something, and struck for the hills, strongly determined that they would not come back to the reservation again.

I was sent to bring them back; they had a week the start of me. I had a good horse, however, and taking with me an Indian boy named Suarki, to lead the pack horse, I started out. The second day we struck their trail, and knowing well the signs they always leave behind them, we followed it easily; but it led us over a hundred and fifty miles through a rough country before we found the runaway band.

On the sixth day we came upon them camped on the Salmon River. We pitched our camp about a hundred yards away. After unsaddling our horses, I went over to have a talk with them.

Old Sagwich was very angry. He said he knew what I was after, but he wouldn't go back; and I would not go back either, for they would fix me so that I couldn't give them any more trouble. He said I ought to be their friend, but instead of that I was helping to bring more trouble to them. The whites he accused of lying to them and robbing them of their hunting ground and forcing them to

Trading post at Fort Hall Indian reservation, Idaho.

Piute Indian girl carrying corn (Southern Utah).

work at something they knew nothing about. They would bear it no longer; they would fight first. The old chief grew angrier as he went on.

"You need not think of escaping this time," he said to me. "We intend to tie you to that tree and burn you alive." I tried to reason with them, telling them I knew I was in their power; but it wouldn't do them any good to kill me. If they did, the soldiers would soon follow and kill the last one of them.

"We are not afraid of the soldiers," he retorted. "We would rather die fighting than starve."

"Well," I replied, "if you kill me, you will kill one of the best friends the Indians ever had."

But nothing I could say seemed to make any difference with old Sagwich. He was determined to carry out his threat. If he had his way I knew he would do it. The other Indians, however, were not so devilish. One of them gave me some fresh elk meat, and I went back to my camp. Things looked rather black for me that night. My only hope was that the other Indians would not stand by old Sagwich.

If the worst came, I had determined to sell my life as dearly as possible. The Indians held a council that night. We kept close watch till morning, but as no one offered to harm us, we began to feel a little easier. After saddling our horses, I told Suarki I was going over to have

Dr. T. M. Bridges

At the Indian agency; squaw with papoose in Indian cradle.

another talk with them, and instructed him that if they made a move to kill me, he should leap on my horse and strike for home to tell the Indian Agent.

Old Sagwich was so sulky he wouldn't even speak to me. The other Indians, however, acted better. They said nothing of what had been decided, but that day they packed up and took the trail towards home. We followed them. On our way down the river we came upon one of the Indians fishing. He told me about the council. Old Sagwich was stubborn in his determination to kill me, but the rest wouldn't consent and he had to give up his bloody plan.

This experience made me feel that my job was too risky for the pay I was getting. The Agent wouldn't raise my wages, so I quit him and went back to my home at Oxford, Idaho.

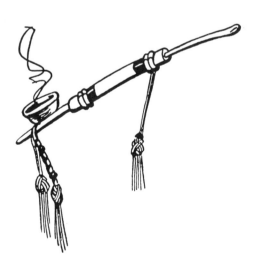

25 FRONTIER TROUBLES

LATER, we moved back into the Bear Lake, where we made our home for twenty years. During this time I was often called on to do dangerous service in the interest of our settlements. After the Indian troubles were over, we had outlaws to deal with who were worse than Indians. For a long time the frontier communities suffered from depredations committed by cattle rustlers and horse thieves. Organized bands operated from Montana to Colorado. They had stations about a hundred miles apart in the roughest places in the mountains. They would often raid our ranges and steal all the cattle and horses they could pick up, driving them into their mountain retreat. They got so daring finally that they even came into the settlements and robbed stores and killed men. The colonists did not get together to stop these outrages till after a fatal raid was made upon Montpelier, when a store was robbed and a clerk was shot dead. This roused the people of the valley to action. Gen. Charles C. Rich called upon the leaders of the towns to send two

men from each settlement — the best men to be had —
to pursue and punish the outlaws. Fourteen men re-
sponded to the call, among them four of the leaders
themselves. It fell to my lot to be one of this posse.

We struck across the mountains east of Bear Lake,
following the trail of the robbers to their rendezvous on
the Big Piney, a tributary of the Green River. We
knew that they had hidden themselves in this country,
for two of the men with us, whose stock had been stolen,
had followed the robbers to their den to recover their
property. Finding the outlaws in such force, they didn't
dare to claim their stolen stock but returned to Bear
Lake for help.

These men led us to the place where they had come
upon the outlaws; but the outlaws had evidently feared
pursuit and moved camp. To hide their tracks they
had driven their wagons up the creek right in the water
for over a mile. Then they had left the creek and driven
up a little ravine and over a ridge. As we rode up this
ravine, to the top of the ridge, the two men who were in
the lead sighted the tepees of the robbers in the hollow
below. They dodged back to keep out of sight, and we
all rode down into the thick willows on the Big Piney, hiding our horses and ourselves among them. The two men
that had sighted the outlaw camp then slipped up the hill
again on foot, secreting themselves in the sagebrush at the
top of the ridge, and watched the rest of the afternoon to
see whether the outlaws had mistrusted anything; but
they showed no sign of having seen us. At dark they
came and reported.

We held council then to decide what plan to pursue to
capture the outlaws. As the robbers outnumbered us,
more than two to one, and were well armed, it was serious
business. Our sheriff weakened when the test came; he

said he couldn't do it, and turned his papers over to Joseph Rich, as brave a man as ever went on such a trip. There were others who felt pretty shaky and wanted to turn back, but Mr. Rich said we had been picked as the best men in Bear Lake and he didn't feel like going back without making an attempt to capture the thieving band. One man said he was ready to go cut the throats of the whole bunch of robbers if the captain said so, but Mr. Rich said, "No; we did not come out to shed blood. We want to take them alive and give them a fair trial."

Every man was given a chance to say how he felt. Most of us wanted to make the attempt to capture the outlaws, and the majority ruled.

How to do it was the next problem. It would have been folly for so few of us to make an open attack on so many well-armed men. The only way we could take them was by surprise, when they were asleep. This plan agreed upon, Mr. Rich proposed that we go down the hill with our horses and pack animals, get in line at the bottom, then, just at the peep of day, charge upon their camp, jump from our horses, run into their tents and grab their guns. When we had decided on this plan of action, Mr. Rich said that this probably meant a fight. If it did we should let them fire first. Should they kill one of us, we must not run; for if we did so they would kill us all. We should give them the best we had. With our double-barreled shotguns loaded with buckshot, we would make things pretty hot for them if they showed fight.

In order that we might know exactly the situation, and have our tents picked out beforehand, so as not to get in a mix-up, two volunteers were called for to go down through their camp in the night and get the lay of things. Jonathan Hoopes and I offered to go. Their tepees were pitched on both sides of a little stream, which was

deep enough for us to keep out of sight by stooping a little.
Down this stream we stole our way, wading with the current so as not to make any noise, till we got right among
the tepees. The biggest one was pitched on the brink of
the stream. We could hear some of the men inside of it
snoring away lustily. Hoopes reached his hand up and
found a blanket on which were some service berries spread
out to dry. Being hungry, we helped ourselves, filling
our pockets with them. After taking in the situation
fully, we slipped back to our boys.

There were seven tents in all, and fourteen of us — two
to each tent. Hoopes and I were to take the largest, the
other boys were assigned theirs. We waited for day to
break; just as it did, the word was given; we popped
spurs to our horses and away we went. A few seconds
and we had leaped from them, rushed into the tents and
begun to grab the guns from the robbers, who, wakened
so rudely, stared stupidly, while we gathered in their
weapons. By the time Hoopes was through passing them
out to me, I had my arms loaded with rifles and revolvers.
Mr. Rich told me to carry them up the hill a piece and
stack them. "Shoot the first man who makes a move
to touch them," was his order. When I looked around,
there sat three of our men on their horses; they hadn't
done their duty, so some of the tents were yet untouched.
I told Hoopes, and he jumped over the creek to one of
them. I was just gathering up some weapons I had
dropped when a big half-breed made a jump at me, grabbed
my shotgun and we had a lively tussle for a few minutes.
He might have got the better of me, for he was a good
deal bigger than I, but Hoopes jumped to the rescue and
cracked him on the head with his revolver so hard that it
knocked him senseless for some time.

When the outlaws rallied themselves enough to sense

what had happened, they broke out of their tents in double-quick time, swearing and cursing and demanding what we wanted.

Captain Rich told them to keep quiet, that they were all under arrest, that we had the advantage, but we would not harm them if they behaved themselves. Seeing that it was useless to resist, they settled down.

The captain then ordered them to kill a calf for us, as we had not had anything to eat since noon the day before. They obeyed orders and we soon had a good breakfast. Later in the day part of our men went out and searched their herds. A good many cattle and horses belonging to our men were found among them.

The leaders of the outlaws were not in this band. They were off making another raid somewhere. One of the band of outlaws was deaf and dumb. Captain Rich took this fellow aside and carried on a conversation with him by writing. From the man he learned that the rest of the band were expected in that night, but as they didn't come, we concluded that they had seen us and were lying off in the hills waiting a chance to ambush us and rescue their comrades. We were too sharp to give them the chance to do that. For three days we waited, guarding our prisoners. Then, as we thought it too risky to try to take so large a band of desperate men through the rough timbered country we must pass to get home, we took forty head of their horses as bond for their appearance at court in thirty days, and let the prisoners go.

When we were ready to set out, we carried their guns to the top of a hill, and Hoopes and I were left to guard the weapons till we were sure our men were far enough away to be safe; then we left the weapons and struck out for home after them.

As no one ever came to redeem the horses, they were

sold at auction. This nest of outlaws was broken up for good the following year. Since then that part of the country has had no serious trouble with horse thieves and robbers.

One more rather exciting experience that befell me and then I shall close these stories of my life in the rugged West.

It happened in 1870. Jim Donaldson, Charley Webster, or "Webb," as we called him, and I were taking a peddling trip to Fort Stanbow, the soldier post that was temporarily established near South Pass for the protection of the miners and emigrants. We had loaded up our three wagons with butter, eggs, and chickens.

The Sioux Indians were then on the warpath. We had been warned to keep an eye on our horses, but we thought little about it till one day we were nooning on the Big Sandy — about where Lot Smith burnt the government wagon trains — when, just as we sat down to eat, "Webb" looked up to see our horses, which we had turned loose to graze, disappearing in a cloud of dust. Two Indians were behind them, both on an old horse of mine, and they were whooping the others across the hills to beat time.

Jumping to our feet we dashed after them afoot. This was useless, of course. "Webb" and Donaldson jerked out their revolvers and took several shots at the rascals, but they were out of revolver reach and getting farther away every second, while we stared and damned them.

It was a pretty pickle we were in — forty miles from nowhere, with three wagons loaded with perishable stuff, and not a horse to move them. We got madder and madder as we watched the thieving devils gradually slip out of sight beyond the sand hills.

Then we went back to our wagons — cussing and discussing the situation. For an hour or more we tried to puzzle a way out of our difficulty. It was no use. The more we worried the worse it looked. All the money I had was invested in those eggs and butter and they would soon be worse than nothing in the hot sun. The other boys were in as bad a fix as I was. We just couldn't see a way out of it; but we kept up our puzzling till suddenly we heard a rumbling noise.

A few minutes later a covered wagon drawn by a pair of mules came in sight.

An old man — "Boss Tweed" the boys had nicknamed him — was the driver. In the seat with him was a boy, who had a saddle horse tied behind. They were surely a welcome sight to us.

We told them of our trouble. The old man reckoned he could help us out. He proposed that we load the supplies of two of our wagons on his larger wagon, then trailing our other wagon behind, his old mules he thought could haul us into South Pass. It looked like our only chance, but "Webb" thought he had a better plan.

The Indians, he said, must make their way out of the country through a certain pass. There was no other route they could escape by. If we three would take the mules and boy's horse and ride hard through the night, we might get ahead of the thieves and retake our horses.

"Anything for the best," said the old man; but the boy objected. We shouldn't take his horse. He started to untie his animal, but we stopped him. Our situation was a desperate one; he had to give in.

We unhitched the mules, and strapped quilts on their backs. Donaldson and I jumped on them; "Webb" took the horse. Then we struck the trail single file, my old mule on lead with Jim to whip him up and "Webb" behind him to whip Jim's mule. It was a funny sight. I never meet Jim but he calls up that circus parade loping along over the hills out on the Big Sandy.

S. N. Leek, Jackson, Wyoming

Unc.e Nick (E. N. Wilson, author of this book), landing a big trout out of Jackson Lake, Wyoming.

The old mules were slow, but they were tough. They kept up their steady gait mile after mile through the night. We couldn't see any trail — just the gap in the mountains against the sky to guide us as we loped and jogged and jogged and loped through the long night.

When daylight came to light our way, we found ourselves at the place where the trail took up over the pass. Soon it forked, the two branches of the trail going up two ravines which were separated by a low, narrow ridge. We saw no fresh tracks on either trail, so we knew the Indians had not passed this point. It looked as if we had got ahead of them as "Webb" hoped.

We rode up one ravine about a mile from the forks, keeping out of the trail so as to leave no tracks to alarm the thieves if they came our way. Here we stopped and "Webb" went up on the ridge to where he could overlook the country and at the same time watch both trails. Our plan was to wait till we found out which trail the Redskins took. Then we could post ourselves on either trail and head them off as they came up the one or the other ravine, it being but a short distance between the trails.

"Webb" had not been on watch long before he sighted them coming about six miles away. He waited till they reached the forks. Luck favored us. They took our trail. Seeing this "Webb" slipped down to tell us. We hastily hid our horses in the tall brush that bordered the little creek, chose a place where the big birches hung over the trail, and got ready. "Webb" and Donaldson, having revolvers, were to take the lead Indian, while with my rifle I was to settle accounts with the other.

We hadn't long to wait till here they came crowding our horses full tilt along the trail. We held ourselves till we had the dead drop on them, then we all fired. My companions both caught their Indian in the head. I took mine right under the arm. Their horses jumped and they both tumbled off so dead they didn't know what struck them. It may seem a cruel thing to do, but we were not going to take any chances.

I never have found any joy in killing Indians. And I never have killed any except when circumstances compelled it; nor have I ever felt like boasting about such bloody work. These rascals certainly deserved what they got. They had stolen all we had and left us in a very serious difficulty. They were Sioux Indians who were escaping from a battle with the soldiers of Fort Stanbow.

You can easily believe we were mighty glad to get back those horses and strike the trail again towards our wagons. We found things all right there. The old man had taken good care of our produce while we were away. He was just as happy as we were over our success. But do you think he would take any pay for his trouble? Not a cent. It was pay enough, he said, to feel so good because he had helped us out of a bad fix. When we got to South Pass, however, we found his home and left him some supplies with our good wishes. He was away at the time, so he couldn't object.

The boy who had refused us his horse didn't object, though, to taking five dollars for his pay. I've always found a heap of difference among the human beings one meets in his travels.

The years that have followed these wild days have not been so filled with exciting adventures, yet no year has passed without its rough and trying experiences; for it has been my lot to live always on the frontier. Even now my home is in Jackson's Hole — one of the last of our mountain valleys to be settled. In 1889 I first went into this beautiful valley, and a few years later I pioneered the little town now called Wilson, in my honor.

It was here that I was brought again into close contact with my Shoshone friends — the Indians from whom for many years I had been all but lost. In 1895, when the so-called Jackson's Hole Indian war broke out and several Indians were killed and others captured and brought to trial for killing game, I was called on to act as interpreter. My sympathies went out to the Indians at this time.

They were misunderstood and mistreated as they always have been. The Indian has always been pushed aside, driven, and robbed of his rights.

It is a sad thought with me to see the Redmen giving away so rapidly before our advancing civilization. Where thousands of the Indians once roamed free, only a scattered few remain. The old friends of my boyhood days with Washakie have almost entirely passed away. Only once in a great while do I find one who remembers Yagaki, the little boy who once lived with their old chief's mother. But when I do happen to meet one — as I did last year when I found Hans, a wealthy Indian, who lives now on his ranch at the Big Bend in Portneuf Canyon — then we have a good time, I tell you, recalling the days of long ago when Uncle Nick was among the Shoshones.

A lily pond in the Yellowstone Park, which was part of the land of the Shoshones.

GLOSSARY

EDITORIAL NOTE. The Indian words and definitions given in this glossary have been carefully checked by a scholar of national reputation, who has studied the Shoshone language. He has pronounced the words as nearly correct as one can represent in our symbols these differing dialects of the Indian tribes. It has been the effort of the editor to be accurate, but it is difficult to give exactly the sounds of the Indian language.

Angitapa (Ăn'gi-tạ-pä'). Name applied by Shoshone Indians to Rock Creek, Idaho.

Antelope (ăn'tĕ-lōp). Animal akin to the deer, a native of the Western plains and open mountain valleys. Commonly called pronghorns. The North American pronghorn is not a true antelope.

Balzamoriza (bäl'zạ-mō-rī-zạ). A species of plant with showy yellow blossoms, and velvety leaves, belonging to sunflower family. Commonly known as "spring sunflower." The seeds were used by Indians for food. It grows about one foot high.

Bannocks (Băn'nŏcks or Pä'nŏoks). Tribe of western Indians allied to Shoshones. Dr. Robert Lowie, of the American Museum of Natural History, gives the name *Banaite* as the one he found applied by the Lemhi Indians to the Bannocks.

Chaps (from Spanish-American chaparajos). Leather or sheepskin leggings worn by cowboys to protect their legs from thorny bushes while riding.

Chief Joseph. Leader of Nez Percé Indians during sixties and seventies, who with Chief Looking-Glass and others led his tribe in a revolt against the United States, and afterwards fled with his people towards Canada, but was overtaken by soldiers under General Miles, captured, and held in this country.

Coyote (kī-ō'te). Animal of the wolf family, a native of Western plains. Picturesquely described by Mark Twain in his *Roughing It.*

Echo Canyon. A canyon about twenty miles in length, leading from southwestern Wyoming westward into Utah. Through this canyon ran the pony express and overland trail. The canyon is so named because of the clear echoes made by its red sandstone cliffs.

Fort Hall. The first Fort Hall was a fur-trading post on the Snake River, about fifteen miles to the north of Pocatello. The second Fort Hall was a military post about fifteen miles to the east of original site. The third and present Fort Hall is on Ross's Fork, about ten miles northeast of Pocatello on Oregon Short-line. Now it is the headquarters of the Indian Agency of that name.

Gosiutes (Gō'shūtes). Name given to scattered bands of Indians living in the deserts of western Utah and eastern Nevada. "Go" in this Indian dialect is said to mean desert or waste place; hence *Gosiutes* would mean desert Utes.

Hanabi (Hăn'a-bi). Washakie's wife.

Hogitsi (Hŏg'ĭt-sĕ). Name of Indian who trapped with Uncle Nick.

Jackson's Hole. One of the splendid valleys in western Wyoming, lying between the Continental divide and the Teton Mountains. It was named after Jackson, an old mountaineer, who made this his rendezvous while trapping and hunting.

Koheets (Kō'heets). Indian name for the curlew (cûr'lew), a Western bird of the plover family. Name given by Indians also to a stream in southern Idaho.

Lemhi (Lĕm'hī). Name given to tribe of Indians and to an early fort or settlement in central eastern Idaho, near the Salmon River. Indian reservation there was abandoned in 1907.

'Lumpy Dick.'' A kind of porridge, made by boiling moistened flour in milk. Used in early days by Western pioneers.

Morogonai (Mōr'ō-gō'nĭ). An old arrow maker and a retired chief of the Shoshones when Uncle Nick lived among them.

Pantsuk (Pănt'sook). Name of Uncle Nick's little Indian brother.

Parowan (Pâr'ō-wăn). Name applied to tribe of Indians in southern Utah. Also name given to first settlement made in the same part of that state.

Piatapa (Pe'ät-a-pä). Name given by Shoshones to Jefferson River, Montana.

Pinto (pĭn'tō). Painted, mottled, or vari-colored. Many of the Indian ponies were pinto ponies. (See pictures on pages 11 and 54.)

Piubi (Pe'ūb-e). Name of one of Washakie's brothers who was killed by snowslide.

Piupa (Pe'ū-pä). Name given to Snake River by Shoshones. Means "Big Water."

Pocatello (Pō'ca tĕl'lō). Name of one of leading chieftains of Shoshones. He did not agree with Washakie in the pacific policy followed by the latter chief. Pocatello protested and fought against the encroachment of the whites. Pocatello, Idaho, was named after this chief.

Quaking aspen. A tree common in the mountains of the West. Named because its leaves are ever trembling. Its bark is white; the tree grows sometimes fifty to sixty feet in height. Its wood is for fuel.

Rawhide. Untanned skin of animals. Strips of this skin were often used in place of ropes and strings by the Indians and pioneers of the West

Sagwich (Săg′wich). A chieftain of Pocatello's band.

Sego (se′gō). A plant of lily family common throughout the mountains and valleys of the West. It grows from a small onion-like bulb, generally found about eight inches in the ground. This bulb was used by the Indians for food. The Utah pioneers, learning of this native food from the Indians, also used it in early days when provisions were scarce. The sego lily has been officially chosen as Utah's State flower. It blooms in the latter part of May, and is used extensively on Decoration Day. Among the interesting spring pastimes of the Western boys and girls are sego digging and gathering sego lilies. Sē′gō is the Indian name for this plant.

Service berries. Small berries similar in size and color to blueberries and huckleberries. Found plentifully in the mountains of the West. They grow on bushes. Used by Indians for food. Granny Pokiboro's service berry basket was among the collection of Shoshone relics pictured on page 111.

Shoshone (Shō′shō-nĕ). Sometimes spelled Shoshoni. Name applied generally to Indians of Utah, Idaho, and Western Wyoming, and some parts of Eastern Nevada. Southern Shoshones were usually spoken of as Ute tribe. "Shoshone" probably means "Snake." The Shoshones were commonly called the Snake Indians by the other tribes and the early pioneers of the West.

Sioux (Sōō). Name of large Indian tribe of the northern central plains.

Sogwobipa (Sŏg-wŏb′bĭ-pä). Name given by Shoshones to Missouri River.

Suarki (Sū-ar′ki). Name of young Indian who accompanied Uncle Nick when he went to bring Sagwich and his band back to the reservation.

Swap (swäp). Means to trade, to exchange.

Tabby (Tăb-by). Tabby means the sun. Name of Gosiute Indian who lived about Grantsville, Utah, in the early days and who saved Uncle Nick. It was also the name of a chief of the Utes.

Tabop (Tă-bŏp′). Letter of recommendation given to Indians. They used such letters at times when they would come asking for food.

Tepee (tē′pēē, also tĭ′pĭ). Name applied to cone-shaped tent used by Western Indian tribes. Made in earlier days of buffalo robes or elk skins; now made of canvas.

Teton Mountains (Tē′tŏn). Name of mountain range on western edge of Wyoming. The Teton Peaks (see picture facing page 1) are famous the world over. The Grand Teton is about 14,000 feet high.

Titsapa (Tĭt′sē-pä). Name given to the Bear River, a stream which rises in northeastern Utah, flows through part of Wyoming and Idaho, and finally finds its way back into Utah and empties into the Great Salt Lake.

Tobitapa (Tō′bĕ-tĭ-pä). Name given by Indians to the Portneuf, a branch of the Snake River. The Portneuf rises in southeastern Idaho and flows through the Portneuf Canyon past Pocatello and empties into the Snake River about ten miles northwest of this city.

Tosaibi (Tō′sĕ-ä′bĭ). Name given springs in southeastern Idaho. The water of these springs is a kind of natural soda water. They are used by many for medicinal purposes. Tosa or Tose means white. The sediment from these springs makes whitish mounds.

Tosenamp (Tō′sē-nămp′). Whitefoot. Tose (white), namp (foot). Name given to Indian who worked for Uncle Nick's father.

Umbaginny (Ŭm′ba̧-jĭn-ny). A Gosiute Indian killed by the whites for cattle stealing in early days.

Washakie (Wäsh′a̧-kē′). Name of chief of the Shoshones from about 1850 until his death about 1890.

Wickiup (wĭck′ĭ-ŭp). Name given to brush huts and other rude shelters built by the Indians out West.

Yagaki (Yă′ga̧-kē). Name given by Indians to Uncle Nick. Means "the crier."

Yaibi (Yĭ′bĭ). Name of one of Washakie's brothers killed by a snowslide.